SITKA

· AND ITS OCEAN / ISLAND WORLD ·

Quarterly
For members of The Alaska Geographic Society
Vol. 9, No. 2 / 1982

The Alaska Geographic Society

To teach many more to better know and use our natural resources

Chief Editor, Robert A. Henning; **Assistant Chief Editor,** Barbara Olds
Editor: Penny Rennick; **Editorial Assistant,** Kathy Doogan; **Cartographer,** Jon.Hersh

Research Editor, this issue: Pat Roppel

Many editors and photographers contributed to this volume. Particular thanks go to
historican-researcher Pat Roppel, of Ketchikan, who spent many long weeks
gathering essential facts and photos and properly deserves the credit line.

ALASKA GEOGRAPHIC®, ISSN 0361-1353, is
published quarterly by The Alaska Geographic
Society, Anchorage, AK 99509. Second-class postage
paid in Anchorage, AK 99509. Printed in Thailand.

THE ALASKA GEOGRAPHIC SOCIETY is a nonprofit organization exploring new frontiers of knowledge across the lands of
the Polar Rim, learning how other men and other countries live
in their Norths, putting the geography book back in the
classroom, exploring new methods of teaching and learning —
sharing in the excitement of discovery in man's wonderful new
world north of 51°16'.

MEMBERS OF THE SOCIETY receive *ALASKA
GEOGRAPHIC®*, a quality magazine that devotes each quarterly
issue to monograhic in-depth coverage of a northern geographic
region or resource-oriented subject.

MEMBERSHIP DUES in The Alaska Geographic
Society are $39 per year; $43 to non-U.S. addresses.
(Eighty percent of each year's dues is for a one-year
subscription to *Alaska Geographic®*.) *Order from
The Alaska Geographic Society, Box 93370,
Anchorage, AK 99509; (907) 258-2515.*

MATERIALS SOUGHT: The editors of *ALASKA GEOGRAPHIC®*
seek a wide variety of informative material on the lands north
of 51°16' on geographic subjects — anything to do with
resources and their uses (with heavy emphasis on quality color
photography) — from all the lands of the Polar River and the
economically related north Polar Rim. We cannot be responsible
for submissions not accompanied by sufficient postage for return
by certified mail. Payments are made for all material upon
publication.

*CHANGE OF ADDRESS: The post office does not
automatically forward Alaska Geographic®* when
you move. To insure continuous service, notify us six
weeks before moving. Send us your new address and
zip code (and moving date), your old address and zip
code, and if possible send a mailing label from a copy
of *Alaska Geographic®*. Send this information to
Alaska Geographic®, Box 93370, Anchorage, AK
99509.

MAILING LISTS: We have begun making our members' names
and addresses available to carefully screened publications and
companies whose products and activities may be of interest to
you. If you would prefer not to receive such mailings, please
so advise us, and include your mailing label (or your name and
address if label is not available).

Library of Congress cataloging in publication data
Main entry under title:

Sitka—and its ocean/island world.

   (Alaska geographic, ISSN 0361-1353; v. 9,
no. 2)
   1. Sitka (Alaska)—Description.   2. Sitka
(Alaska)—History.   3. Sitka region (Alaska)—
Description and travel.   4. Sitka region (Alaska)—
History.   I. Alaska geographic.   II. Alaska
Geographic Society.   III. Series.
F901.A266 vol. 9, no. 2   (F914.S6)979.8'2   82-1752
ISBN 0-88240-168-8   AACR2

The cover: Background photo, a wake from the purse seiner *Alsek* (Mary Henrickson).
Inserts top to bottom; Totem (Dianne Hofbeck, staff). St. Michaels Cathedral (Sharon Paul, staff).
Russian blockhouse (Nancy Simmerman).
Title page — From viewpoints around Sitka, one can look out on the tiny islands of Sitka
Sound, and beyond to the broad sweep of the North Pacific. Russians named the sound
after a Tlingit Indian word, which some sources translate to mean "by the sea." (Ernest Manewal)

The subject "Sitka" has long been tantalizing to us editors of *ALASKA GEOGRAPHIC®*, but one difficult to embrace. It is "history" . . . it is "Tlingit" . . . it is "Russian" . . . it is "Fish" . . . "Fur" . . . and modern history that is part national American and part straight Alaska.

Sitka is also not just Sitka itself, in its own peculiar local beauty and historic romance. It is also to a large degree much of Chichagof Island and Baranof Island for which it is and has been in the past a trading center to one degree or another. Although Juneau to the northwest, Petersburg to the east, and Ketchikan to the southeast have also traded with various other communities and facilities that developed over the years on Baranof and Chichagof, all of these communities were somehow more in the Sitka orbit. At the very beginnings, Sitka was certainly center for Southeast Alaska commerce, and also the only real city on the entire American west coast.

So this volume of The Alaska Geographic Society will try to give you not a historical sketch of Sitka . . . but a feel for this fascinating land and an appreciation of its place in time . . . from the days of flint to the frightful miracle of the atom.

A place of unusual charm, unusual beauty.

The Editors

Left — The quiet fishing village of Elfin Cove has only 28 year-round residents. The town offers a protected anchorage near the largest salmon fishing banks in Southeast Alaska, the Fairweather Grounds. (Matt Donohoe)

Above — Indian River, about a mile southeast of Sitka, was originally named Koloshian River, after ''Kolosh,'' the Russian name for the local tribe of Tlingit Indians. (Stephen E. Hilson)

Left — Crescent Harbor, one of several boat harbors in Sitka, is home for a fairly large fleet of fishing boats. Two cold storage facilities in the city process salmon, halibut, black cod and herring. (Ueli Ackermann)

Overleaf — The waters of Shelikof Bay, on the west coast of Kruzof Island, reflect the sunset. (Ernest Manewal)

Glacier Bay
Lemesurier Island
Icy Strait
Point Adolphus
Alaska State Ferry
Hoonah

Inian Island
Elfin Cove

Cross Sound
Cape Bingham

Pelican
Yakobi Island
Lisianski Inlet
Lisianski Strait
Idaho Inlet
Port Frederick
Game Creek
Freshwater Bay

Admiralty Island
Admiralty Island National Monument

ALASKA

Map Location

Chichagof Island

White Sulphur Springs
West Chichagof-Yakobi Wilderness

Tenakee Inlet
Tenakee

Moore

Mountains

Chatham

N

Scale
30 miles
30 kilometers

Hill Island
Hogan Island
Herbert Graves Island
Khaz Bay

Moser Island

Freeburn Mountain 3,252'
Pinnacle Peak 3,215'

Peril Strait

Catherine Island

Khaz Peninsula

Alaska State Ferry

Salisbury Sound

Partofshikof Island

Halleck Island

Baranof Island

Baranof
Warm Springs Bay

Krestof Island

Kruzof Island

Old Sitka

Harbor Peak 2,193'

The Sisters 3,880'
Mount Verstovia 3,300'

Kupreanof Island

Shelikof Bay

Sitka

Sitka Sound

Alaska State Ferry

Mount Edgecumbe 3,201'
Saint Lazaria Island
National Wildlife Refuge

Cape Edgecumbe

Biorka Island

Goddard

Redoubt Lake

South Baranof Wilderness

Kuiu Island

Kuiu Island

Rakof Islands

Whale Bay

Maksoutof River

Little Port Walter

Port Alexander

Cape Ommaney

SITKA

·AND ITS OCEAN/ ISLAND WORLD·

Sitka, one of Alaska's most historic cities, and certainly a city situated in one of the North's most spectacularly beautiful settings, was at one time truly the "Capital of the Pacific" . . . Chicago was just a blockhouse in a swamp and San Francisco was still a sleepy mission, when Sitka was a bustling center of North Pacific commerce. Founded in 1799, destroyed by the local Indians in 1802, rebuilt by Alexander Andreievich Baranov in 1804, Russian until Alaska's sale to the United States in 1867, Sitka is as Sitka was . . . a place where the sea boils and surges

Opposite — Mount Verstovia (3,300 feet) dominates the skyline above Sitka. The Sitka Pioneers' Home is the red-roofed building near the center of the photo; Saint Michael's Cathedral is to the right. (Sharon Paul, staff)

Stately trees, mostly spruce, hemlock and cedar, tower over most of Baranof and Chichagof islands, providing lush settings as well as employment opportunities in the logging industry.
(Chip Porter)

out of the empty horizon to the West, where Indian and white man still live together, taking their livelihoods from the sea and the forest, and where the history of the centuries is yet evident all around, and the magic of life is accentuated by the timeless beauty of the land.

A festoon of little islands, some large, many small, most covered like jade necklace pieces with the green of spruce and hemlock, some just bare rocks upon which the sea lions haul out, and the ceaseless surf, sometimes rising only softly and slightly against the rocky shores, sometimes crashing in the full fury of North Pacific storm, protects the Sitka anchorage and shorefront.

Deep green rain forests, rich in lush vegetation and rushing streams, are the most typical type of terrain at lower elevations of Baranof and Chichagof islands. (Matt Donohoe)

Left — Fluffy clouds reflect on the still water of Lisianski Inlet, looking west from Pelican. The Fairweather Range is barely visible in the distance. (Chip Porter)

Behind Sitka the green forests rise swiftly to a timberline at around 2,000 feet. Nearby peaks, like Verstovia, 3,300 feet, the Sisters, 3,880 feet, with snow and ice among the pinnacles, and Harbor Peak on the north, 2,193 feet, make lovely backdrop. The intermittent and underlying brush make these forests in some places almost impenetrable. Trails are few, and the knowing make their way to the higher slopes with local knowledge of intersecting muskegs and steep brushless clear timber stands here and there. And the forest is more often wet than dry for this is the first of the Southeast Alaska Alexander Archipelago to catch the moisture laden weather moving in off the open ocean from the South Pacific. Sitka receives around 90 inches of precipitation a year, and like most of coastal Alaska, "You pay your money and you take your choice" as to when it is all "driest and best." It may rain for days, and it may cook in the sun and the creeks will dry up for as many days at another time. The weather and the land itself together create both challenge and fascination.

But Sitka is not just a sanctuary for the sailor behind the protecting island screen and a headquarters town for around 8,000 people largely supported by the income from a local pulp mill and the landings of a large fishing fleet. It is in the larger sense a central point for a sea and island world that embraces not only the surf battered string of outer islands, but the entire Baranof Island upon which Sitka sits, and its economic and physical neighbor to the north, Chichagof Island, the

Above — Sitka spruce, western hemlock and Alaska cedar dominate the forests surrounding Sitka.
(Ernest Manewal)

Opposite — Low light illuminates part of the fleet and the fish house where fishermen sell their catch at Port Alexander, a small fishing community on the southern tip of Baranof Island. The port has two docks, this one called the Front Float, and another farther back in the more protected part of the harbor called the Back Float.
(Tom Paul)

13

A row of old houses lines the waterfront of Sitka Harbor in this view from Japonski Island. Sitka has a rich and colorful past, and its residents take pride in preserving and restoring the city's historical landmarks. (Ernest Manewal)

Right — The distinctive contour of Mount Edgecumbe (3,201 feet), one of the best known landmarks of Southeast Alaska, dominates the horizon west of Sitka. Edgecumbe, located on Kruzof Island, is an extinct volcano which probably last erupted 10,000 to 11,000 years ago. (Stephen E. Hilson)

two islands together with their smaller satellite islands representing the northern and outer islands of the greater Southeast Alaska system that is for the most part made up of many other islands in the Alexander Archipelago to the east and south which in turn are backdropped by the massive Coastal Range with its deep fjords and vast ice fields.

Dominating the Sitka harbor scene and the Baranof-Chichagof Mountains connecting those two (locally called "The Baranofs"), is yet another, but different peak . . . the truncated cone of 3,201-foot-high Mount Edgecumbe, a long-extinct volcano on Kruzof Island, 16 miles to the west of Sitka. In the early summer months, when snow reaches far down Mount Edgecumbe's slopes, the likeness to Japan's famous Mt. Fujiyama is readily apparent. Behind Edgecumbe, hidden from Sitka view, is yet another old volcano with over half of its top blown off in what must have been a tremendous long ago explosion. Together with a number of other cinder cones in the immediate area here on Kruzof Island just off the Baranof and Chichagof shores is one of the few evidences in Southeast Alaska of volcanic disturbance. This area is now long quiescent and little seen by visitors. A Forest Service trail leads seven miles from Fred's Creek to the summit and like other trails and other places of charm for the visitor in this region, only boat or aircraft charter make them attainable.

Modern man in this area was the Tlingit Indian, who, from the old handed-down stories of the elders, apparently came down the few mountain cutting great rivers like the Stikine and the Nass and the high Chilkat passes to the north, trickle migrations from what apparently was a much greater migration of peoples over an indeterminate number of years crossing the Bering Land Bridge from Asia, following the game herds and perhaps the weather behind the coastal mountains to settle eventually up and down the length of what is now the western United States and Mexico. The Navajos of the American Southwest speak a root language from which also came that of the Sitka Tlingit.

Sitka was a big Indian village, both in summer and winter, but in summer, numbers of families scattered to various fishing sites which they "possessed" in a tribal sense of property recognition as binding then as patents and real estate documents of today. On the north island of this Indian world was another great village, Hoonah . . . another Tlingit tribe . . . and on Admiralty Island, to the east across Chatham Strait separating Admiralty and other islands from Baranof and Chichagof, was another important village and tribal branch in this Tlingit world . . . the people of Angoon. But the dividing lines between tribes and between families were binding things known to all and respected by all. There was visiting back and forth, but little warring here. That was confined largely (and long ago) to tribal groups to the south.

Recently, to further deepen the mysteries of this land, archaeologists

have discovered the old campfires and tools of a truly ancient people that in successive settlings and resettlings of at least one primitive camp in between resurgent ice ages, dates back perhaps 10,000 years. This site, only a score of airline miles across Baranof Island east of Sitka, found by workmen while constructing a fish hatchery on Kasnyku Bay in 1978, offers tantalizing possibilities that other such sites and more knowledge will be revealed.

Life for the early Tlingit was probably as close to the ideal as that enjoyed by any aboriginals of long ago . . . plenty of fish of all kinds in the sea, shellfish on the beaches, and deer in the forests. There was seldom any lack of food although old stories tell of surviving starvation periods of heavy snows and cold by pounding and eating the inner bark of hemlock and other trees. But by and large there was much food almost everywhere, furs for warmth, plenty of timber for shelter and fire. The fine dugout canoes these people made and together with the natural visiting habits of clans and tribes, further resulted in much trading back and forth for that which either lacked. There was jade, for example, probably from the British Columbia Haidas and other tribes. There were mountain goat skins and wool from tribes near to the mainland mountain fastnesses where these high denizens live. There were even the occasional copper things from the Copper River people far to the North, and persistently, quite early, without adequate records from what traders they came, iron knives and iron axes.

Later, as more and more sailing and trading white men explorers discovered this Tlingit (and Aleut) world of furs and riches, more guns and salt and calico . . . and disease, were also traded. The Time of The White Man had arrived.

The Russians "discovered" Alaska in 1741 . . . (The Tlingits would argue that point, as perhaps would their forebears of some 10,000 years earlier.) . . . and in their pursuit of fur riches followed the furs and the trappers from the Aleutians up the Alaska Peninsula to Kodiak and Cook Inlet . . . and up through Bristol Bay and along the Bering Sea littoral . . . even up the great Yukon and Kuskokwim Rivers . . . and east and south along the Gulf of Alaska to found the hub city and the nadir of their Pacific expansion, Sitka.

Traders and explorers from England, from New England, even early on from Spain, out of Mexico, and from far away France also "discovered" Alaska . . . and Sitka. Long before the priests of California had made their missions more than adobe fortresses in the wilderness, shipyards and foundries and merchant outfitters were busy in Sitka. The Russians traded with all, and reached out for more colonies and trade as far south as Fort Ross, California, as far south and west as the Hawaiian Islands, but wars and politics and declining fur populations brought more than a century of Russian adventures in what is now Alaska to an end.

In 1867 the Russian flag came down and an American flag went up at Sitka. There followed many years of

Above — A ceremonial rattle is depicted in this detail of a totem pole raised in front of the Visitor's Center at Sitka National Historical Park in 1976 to commemorate 200 years of Northwest Coast Indian history. The rattle represents the rich ceremonial culture of the early Indians. (Dianne Hofbeck, staff)

Right — Tourism generates a substantial portion of Sitka's revenue. Many visitors arrive during the summer months aboard cruise ships and Alaska Marine Highway ferries. (Mary Henrikson)

bungling political and military administration . . . Alaska was in a sense as far from American headquarters in Washington as the Russians had been from Moscow . . . and there were many I-told-you-so's who declaimed that Seward, the Secretary of State most directly responsible for the purchase of Alaska, really had indulged a "folly."

But Alaska . . . and Sitka . . . awoke with the Klondike gold rush . . . (the story of any land frontier "development" somehow always seems to swing on the opportunities for new wealth.) . . . and after the gold seekers came the cannerymen. When the Hume Brothers began canning the fat king salmon of the Sacramento River in 1864, a mad scramble began to cash in on the silver hordes of salmon that crowded rivers and bays from San Francisco to Kotzebue.

Within a few years of Alaska's purchase, the cannerymen arrived. In 1878, Sitka was the scene of one of the first two canning ventures in Alaska (the other at Klawock on Prince of Wales Island). The salmon boom lasted in varying degree, depending on markets and the size of runs until the first dams began to ruin the spawning beds of the Columbia, that great mother stream to a large proportion of North Pacific salmon. Runs gradually diminished and have never returned to early grandeur if the principal run stock was Columbia born. There should be a R.I.P. King Salmon tablet atop the first of those 1930s Columbia dams.

Russians were not miners. An occasional geologist type found mild inter-

17

Trollers and longliners are tied to the float at Pelican, a fishing village on the west side of Chichagof Island. The island's relatively low but rugged peaks rise in the background. (Chip Porter)

Right — The west coast of Chichagof Island, facing the open Pacific, has some of the most rugged, surf-battered country in Southeast Alaska. (Ernest Robertson)

est in Cook Inlet coal seams, a bit of placer gold, here and there, but when the Russian fur business went sour there was no consideration apparently that there was more to their Sitka and Alaska based ventures than furs alone. Not long after the Russians accepted their flag back, Sitka prospectors found gold at what became Juneau . . . and because of the resulting shift in metropolitan prosperity likewise lost their capital city status. Paradoxically, Juneau now rests in imminent peril of in turn losing the capital to Willow, not far from Anchorage, today's epicenter of new wealth . . . oil now instead of gold instead of fur.

Between the gold and the oil Sitka had another chapter in its history. When World War II broke out, a lot of politicians, admirals and generals, brushed up on their geography. One of the first results was a Navy patrol base at Sitka . . . military quarters, repair and fuel facilities, guns on the islands, guns on the surrounding peaks. Sitka would never again be the same. Alaska's first military spending boom had struck.

After the military left, with few fish compared to earlier abundance, Sitka again "rested" . . . many of its long ago Russian buildings still intact . . . the onion dome of the Orthodox church still gleaming in the occasional sun . . . and then the Japanese returned . . . with dollars this time instead of guns . . . and with the hands of Washington turned out in welcome instead of fisted in anger as they had been only a few years back . . . Sitka received a modern pulp plant and a fresh new measure of progress and prosperity.

Thanks to a complex combination of political events and Congressional act, Alaska's native people have now received title to vast acreages in Alaska, along with rights to timber and mineral wealth, and the descendants of the Kolosh tribal chiefs who once drove Baranov's people from their fort and in turn were again subdued to hunt and fish largely as the white man desired, now sit on the board of directors of the pulp plant, and are once again chiefs and their people are no longer subject.

An old Sitka has been reborn a new Sitka.

But the sun still glints on the onion dome of Saint Michael's Cathedral, the surf still comes welling in from the vastness of the Pacific, and Sitka is yet a place where men gather in a fascinating and beautiful sea and island world.

Robert A. Henning

Robert A. Henning
President,
Alaska Geographic Society

The Sitka district encompasses Baranof, Chichagof, Yakobi and Kruzof islands and innumerable small islands and islets covering approximately 4,500 square miles. Baranof and Chichagof islands, which form a land mass gradually tapering southeast and separated into two parts only by narrow Peril Strait, contain the majority of this land. Lisianski Strait cuts Yakobi Island, northwest corner of the land mass, from Chichagof Island. With an average width of about 30 miles, the Baranof-Chichagof complex extends for about 150 miles from Point Adolphus at the northern end of Chichagof to Cape Ommaney at the southern tip of Baranof.

Permanent towns are few. Baranof Island has only Sitka, Port Alexander and a tiny settlement at Baranof (Warm Springs Bay). On Chichagof Island are Tenakee Springs, Hoonah, Mount Bether, Elfin Cove and Pelican. A few people live year-round in remote bays scattered throughout the area.

The Baranofs rise abruptly from the shore, in many places forming bold cliffs hundreds of feet high, surmounted by precipitous slopes rising 2,000 to 3,000 feet. These mountains are characterized by sharp pinnacles and comblike ridges, the result of ice erosion only slightly modified by later stream erosion. A rugged, symmetrical range reaching altitudes of 4,500 feet, the Baranof's eastern slopes are extremely steep with gentler slopes to the

This panoramic view shows island-studded Sitka Sound, near sunset. On the right are Mount Edgecumbe and the towers of O'Connell Bridge to Japonski Island.
(Ueli Ackermann)

21

southwest angling from mid-range to shoreline. Winding, steep-sided glacial troughs dissect these slopes and small, regressing glaciers occupy their upper reaches.

The Chichagof Island highlands consist of northwest-trending ridges lower in elevation than on Baranof Island. Dramatic rocky spires and narrow, sharp ridges are visible for miles. Peaks such as Pegmatite Mountain (3,811 feet), Pinnacle Peak (3,215 feet) and Freeburn Mountain (3,252 feet) are typical of the rugged and jagged land forms in the island's northern section.

Present glaciation on the islands is a vanishing remnant of the former greatly extended glaciation which covered this geologically young land. The deeply indented, fiordlike characteristic of many of the waterways is the most immediate evidence of former glaciation which covered Southeast Alaska during the Pleistocene. Nunataks, peaks which rise above the icy expanse, are distinguished by their great altitudes, steep slopes, jagged ridges and sharp, frost-riven peaks. Moving ice eroded the surface and produced round, smooth land forms, even though well-formed cirques are not as common as might be expected for an area that has been so recently and intensively glaciated. However, many streams, particularly those that flow from relatively high areas, head in glacial cirques that contain lakes. Rushing mountain streams are numerous and, because of heavy rainfall, are large compared to their drainage basins.

Volcanism as well as glaciation has influenced the present landscape. The most conspicuous evidence of this molten force is the truncated volcanic cone, Mount Edgecumbe, Alaska's most easterly volcano. Scientists estimate that Mount Edgecumbe (3,201 feet) last erupted 10,000 to 11,000 years ago. The mountain is part of a volcanic field which

Far left — Alpine tundra covers the slopes above Port Alexander, on the southern end of Baranof Island. In the distance is a Sitka black-tailed deer, one of the island's animal inhabitants. (Loyal Johnson)

Left — Low, mat-forming vegetation grows on the tundra surrounding Lake Rosenberg, on Baranof Island. This type of plant life survives the snow and wind of winter and blooms during the short, warm summer season. (R.E. Johnson)

Topography of Baranof and Chichagof islands shows much evidence of the extensive glaciation which covered Southeast Alaska during the Pleistocene. A few remnants of that epoch remain today, such as this unnamed glacier on eastern Baranof Island. (R.E. Johnson)

23

formed during the Pleistocene and Holocene epochs and covers about 104 square miles on the southern end of Kruzof Island and extends to Saint Lazaria Island. The field consists of gently dipping flows, composite cones and air-fall ash and lapilli (small pieces of frothy lava). No other known volcanic action is evident on Baranof and Chichagof islands.

Western portions of Chichagof and Yakobi islands form the West Chichagof-Yakobi Wilderness area of Tongass National Forest, approximately 265,000 acres of rugged shore-line, craggy offshore islands, protected bays and steep mountains.

A second wilderness area has been set aside on South Baranof Island. High mountains rising from sea level to above 4,000 feet char-

acterize South Baranof Wilderness of about 314,000 acres. Numerous waterfalls cascade from the steep slopes to enter long, winding fiords.

Climate of the Baranof-Chichagof islands area is dominated by maritime weather patterns, with variations resulting from topographic features. Wind channeling, an effect of the mountainous terrain, causes moderate to strong south or southeasterly winds with an average annual wind speed of eight to ten knots. Temperatures are mild, ranging from the 40s to mid-60s in summer, and from the high teens to low 40s in winter. Daily temperature changes are small, usually ranging less than 10° F. Precipitation, either in the form of rain or snow, is almost an everyday occurrence throughout the area. Little Port Walter, the wettest spot in Alaska, receives an average of 221 inches of precipitation a year, including 123 inches of snow (one inch of water equals ten inches of snow, meaning approximately 209 inches of the area's precipitation is in the form of rain). Annual precipitation at Pelican, on Chichagof Island, averages 123 inches, 106 inches of which are snow, and the city of Sitka receives an average of 97 inches of precipitation, including 50 inches of snow.

Stretching to eight inches, mountain harebells cling to a lichen-covered rock on the rugged shore of Baranof Island. (Tom Paul)

Even on a short walk hikers can, in season, find hillsides covered with blueberries, huckleberries, or, as shown here, red and gold salmonberries. All can be eaten directly from the bush or made into delicious jams and jellies. (Frank Shoemaker)

Sitka spruce and western hemlock, mixed with a scattering of Alaska cedar, make up the dark-green rain forest, interspersed with open muskeg, that blankets the mountains from sea level to alpine altitudes. Lodgepole pine grow on poorly drained sites. Dwarf mountain hemlock is often associated with muskegs and southern alpine areas. Alders line some streams and many shorelines, dominating landslides and recently logged areas.

Thick, lush undergrowth is common in the forest, and shrubs such as blueberry, huckleberry, devil's club, rusty menziesia, red elder and salal are common. Salmonberry is also quite abundant, reaching heights of six feet on some of the smaller, outer islands. Frequent rainfall makes this undergrowth continuously wet. Mosses grow in great profusion on the ground, on fallen logs, on lichen-draped branches of trees and in forest openings. An array of wild flowers in pinks, blues, reds, whites and yellows bloom from spring until fall.

Sphagnum mosses, grasses, sedges, heaths, Labrador tea and a minuscule pink pincushion called honeydew produce a wet, spongy ground cover. Muskegs vary in size from small pockets where drainage has been retarded to broad expanses.

Alpine tundra lies above 2,500- to 3,000-foot elevations. Soils are generally thin, and resident plants have adapted to snow pack and wind abrasion by evolving into low, mat-forming vegetation. During summer months, cushionlike plants occupy crevices on exposed rock outcrops. Mosses in greens, varying from dark to chartreuse, intermingle with shades of yellow to give the illusion of a velvet covering on the otherwise barren slopes.

Above — Water flowing out of Deer Lake sends spray flying as it cascades over a precipice above Mist Cove, about 19 miles north of Port Alexander at the west entrance to Patterson Bay. (Tom Paul)

Frequent rainfall and warmer temperatures encourage the growth of a wide variety of wild flowers.

Clockwise from right —

■ Yellow pond lily *(Nuphar polysepalum).*

■ Wild geranium *(Geranium erianthum).*

■ Fireweed *(Epilobium augustifolium).*

■ Dwarf dogwood *(Cornus canadensis),* flowering stage.

■ Dwarf dogwood *(cornus canadensis),* berry stage.

(Ernest Manewal)

(Loyal Johnson)

(Ernest Manewal)

(Patricia Roppel)

(Ernest Manewal)

29

The rich and varied vegetation combines with saltwater and freshwater environments to support abundant wildlife on the beaches in the water and in the air.

Monarchs of the skies over Baranof and Chichagof are the bald eagles that soar on extended wings using thermals to gain altitude to hunt or scavenge. Eagles nest in tall, old-growth timber near shorelines. Shorebirds, great blue herons and surface-feeding ducks probe quiet backwaters of intertidal zones and deltas. Trumpeter and whistling swans occasionally visit tidal marshes. The Vancouver Canada goose remains over winter to forage on plant and animal life at tideline near small stream mouths which stay open when tide flats and deltas become ice-covered. In winter, inlets on the east and south end of Baranof Island generally freeze so relatively few birds winter there. However, other bays do not freeze, thus providing suitable winter habitat. For example, Nakwasina Sound, between Baranof Island and the east coast of Halleck Island 11 miles north of Sitka, is an especially good wintering area for scoters and other diving ducks.

Fifty-six seabird colonies are identified in Southeast Alaska; several in the Necker Islands and one on Saint Lazaria Island, lie on the outer fringes of Baranof Island. Rookeries are most often located on steep, rocky headlands or small, rocky islands and islets that furnish refuge from predators yet provide easy ocean access for adult birds and their young. In addition, some non-colonial species such as jaegers, shearwaters and albatrosses are present in offshore waters.

No, it's not three men in a boat — it's three horned puffins on a rock at Round Island in Bristol Bay. These comical-looking birds, sometimes called parrots of the sea, nest in rock crevices, sea cliffs, and on grassy slopes, often standing at attention like colorful little soldiers at the entrances of their burrows. (Tom Bledsoe, reprinted from *ALASKA*® magazine)

Opposite — Saint Lazaria, designated a national wildlife refuge, is located in Sitka Sound, about 15 miles southwest of Sitka. (Stephen E. Hilson)

Below — This eagle is about to snatch a herring, which it spotted swimming near the surface. (Ernest Manewal)

Twenty-one species of birds, including glaucous-winged gulls (below) and black oystercatchers (left), breed within Saint Lazaria National Wildlife Refuge, about 15 miles southwest of Sitka. (Both by Matt Donohoe)

Right — Tide pools and rocky terrain of Saint Lazaria National Wildlife Refuge provide the proper environment for the 21 different species of birds that breed within the refuge. (Matt Donohoe)

Saint Lazaria, a 65-acre island of volcanic origin at the entrance to Sitka Sound approximately 15 miles southwest of Sitka, has been set aside as a national wildlife refuge since 1909. Millions of birds of 21 different species breed here. Burrowing seabirds — tufted puffins; rhinoceros auklets; ancient murrelets; and more than 600,000 storm-petrels, both Leach's and fork-tailed — find the refuge ideal. Saint Lazaria is believed to have the world's largest concentration of storm-petrels. Common and thick-billed murres, pelagic cormorants, glaucous-winged gulls, pigeon guillemots and others inhabit the sea cliffs, while song and fox sparrows and hermit thrushes flit among the lush growth. Two rocky summits rise 100 to 200 feet above the Pacific surf, but the island's upper reaches are gentle and densely vegetated with brush, spruce and hemlock. A thick, almost impenetrable mass of salmonberries, growing as high as a man's head, hinder foot travel on the island. Small boats can land on the island only at high tide and then only with great difficulty because of constant swells from the open ocean. To protect breeding birds and their fragile nesting burrows, the U.S. Fish & Wildlife Service requires special permits to visit the island during breeding season. Saint Lazaria remained uninhabited and apparently seldom visited until a World War II military outpost was established for a brief time there. Remains of the outpost are difficult to find because of the lush vegetation; the metal is corroding and the wood rotting rapidly in the mild, wet climate.

Mink and land otter have been reported on Saint Lazaria. Although brown bear do not regularly inhabit the island, records indicate that these huge mammals do occasionally swim over from Kruzof Island, one and one-half miles to the north.

A cormorant is perched atop its nest among the rocks on Saint Lazaria Island. In addition to birds, the island's inhabitants also include mink, land otter and an occasional brown bear. (Stephen E. Hilson)

Left — A common murre rookery is located on one of Saint Lazaria's steep cliffs. Millions of birds inhabit the 65-acre island. (Stephen E. Hilson)

Mink, otters and bears are common on Baranof and Chichagof islands. Brown bears seem most at home on open grasslands and sedge flats. In the spring, grass and other early herbaceous plants make up the bulk of their diet. By summer, the bears feed on a variety of berries and shrubs. These bulky animals frequent salmon streams in summer and early fall where they join the bald eagles in feasting on spawning salmon. Black bears are not indigenous to these islands.

Shy, but curious Sitka black-tailed deer were not present on Baranof and Chichagof islands until after the Pleistocene ice receded. Alpine terrain is their most important summer range. When snow covers the high country, deer concentrate at low elevations adjacent to tidewater where they feed on dead beach grass, sedges, kelp and scattered pockets of edible brush.

Wolves, one of the predators common to deer on other islands of Southeast, are not found on Baranof and Chichagof islands, or on neighboring Admiralty Island.

One small rodent is believed to be unique to these two islands. The brown and fairly large Sitka mouse, a variation of the common deer mouse, is seldom seen but is abundant in the forest.

Not all wildlife found on Baranof and Chichagof islands is native. The land recently exposed by receding glaciers offered an apparent abundance of unfilled ecological niches which man was obsessed with filling. Consequently, mountain goats, pine martens, raccoons and ring-necked pheasants were introduced to the islands.

At home among wind-worn rocks and alpine meadows lying at or above timber line, mountain goats were captured near Tracy Arm on the Southeast mainland and released on Baranof Island. Up in the rugged and

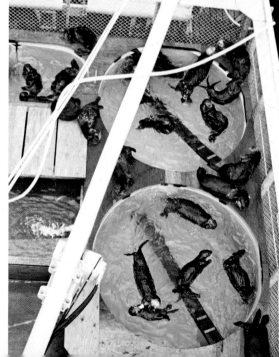

34

Left — Sitka black-tailed deer inhabit the islands, spending summers in the mountains and winters at lower elevations. (Ernest Robertson)
Inset — A Sitka black-tailed fawn hides in new growth at the edge of a forest.
(Loyal Johnson)

Below — Marten were introduced to Baranof Island in 1934 and to Chichagof Island in the early 1950s. It takes about one and a half square miles of land to support one marten. (R. Vallion)

Far left — Sea otters, such as this young one feeding on mussels, once were common along the rugged outer coast of Yakobi, Chichagof, Kruzof, and Baranof islands. However, by the 19th century these animals had been hunted to extinction near Sitka. (Paul Arneson)
Far left bottom — Sea otters feed, swim and rest in holding tanks aboard the *G.B. Reed* during a transplant. In 1966 20 otters were transplanted to Khaz Bay; three years later an additional 58 sea otters were sent to the same bay on Chichagof's outer coast.
(Karl Schneider, ADF&G)

broken terrain of cliffs, ledges, crags and talus slopes, mountain goats quickly adapted to their new home. Populations grew, and in 1950 a hunting season was established. Mountain goats are hunted yearly by hardy sportsmen who have the stamina to climb the mountain peaks.

Because of this success, officials attempted to transplant goats to Chichagof Island. Over the years occasional sightings of goats have been reported, but it is believed few, if any, remain today.

The two most successful furbearer transplants were those of the red squirrel and the pine marten. Despite release of only seven marten, that species began to flourish on Baranof Island. Following this success, 15 marten were released on Chichagof Island several years later, establishing an important population which has spread to the seaward islands.

Red squirrels, first introduced because they were thought to be an important food source for the martens, rapidly adapted to their new home, and today these scampering, curious mammals are seen on many parts of Baranof, Chichagof and neighboring islands.

Two other furbearers did not fare so well. A small beaver population was established on Baranof Island for a number of years. These animals were descended from 10 beavers captured on Prince of Wales Island and released near Goddard Hot Springs in 1927. However, in recent years only a few beaver are known to remain.

Raccoons were released or escaped from Japonski Island resulting in a small population that spread to nearby Baranof Island. No sightings have been reported in recent years.

Not all of man's tamperings with wildlife populations produced results. Sportsmen encouraged introduction of ring-necked pheasants to Baranof Island. This was an outstanding example of failure. Another failure was an attempt to place elk on Kruzof Island in the 1920s. There was talk of grazing 100 head of reindeer on Yakobi Island, but this did not come to fruition.

Efforts to reintroduce sea otters to their traditional home along the rugged outer coastline of Yakobi, Chichagof, Kruzof and Baranof islands were successful. This coastal region once supported a large population of this species, but all were exterminated by commercial fur hunters in the 19th century. Between 1965 and 1969, 272 sea otters were transplanted along the coast near the Necker Islands, south of Lisianski Strait and in Khaz Bay.

Pods of sea otters in Khaz Bay and along Yakobi have shown high reproductive rates and are now well established. A rare treat is to sight one of these graceful mammals floating on its back, eating, washing or dozing in a bed of kelp beside surf-washed rocks.

Left and right — Brown bears are common on Baranof and Chichagof islands, frequenting salmon streams in summer and early fall. (left, Ernest Robertson; right, Tom Munson)

Far right — Red squirrels, introduced onto the islands in 1930 and 1931 because they were thought to be an important food source for martens, readily adapted to their new environment. Today they are a common sight on Baranof and Chichagof islands. (John Johnson)

Harbor seals and Steller sea lions also call these rocks home. Rookeries are scattered all along the outer coast. Other sea mammals such as Dall and harbor porpoises, killer whales, and humpback and other great whales frequent the straits, sound and channels on both the outer coast and the eastern side of the islands.

The ocean waters teem with fish including halibut, numerous species of bottom fish and salmon. These salmon — sockeye, chum, pink and coho — spawn in the many streams which wind through the rain forests. No known spawning streams for chinook salmon exist on Baranof or Chichagof, although many are taken in local waters by trollers.

Streams and lakes are numerous, and many support steelhead, rainbow and cutthroat trout and Dolly Varden.

Colorful sea life covers the ocean floor. Dungeness, tanner and king crab; butter clams, Little Neck clams, and a few razor clams; rock scallops, abalone, sea urchins, octopus and sea cucumbers are just a few.

Left — Sea lions bask on Eagle Rocks, off the west coast of Baranof Island. Largest of the eared seals, sea lion bulls reach up to 13 feet in length and can weigh up to 2,400 pounds. (Stephen E. Hilson)

Right — Unconcerned with the rain, John Stein nets a trout in a small stream near Lake Eva, on the north coast of Baranof Island. (Stephen E. Hilson)

Far right — A stream on Chichagof Island teems with pink salmon. Many streams on both islands are spawning grounds for several species of salmon — sockeye, chum, pink, and coho. (R.E. Johnson)

Right — Dense kelp beds are common along the rocky shores of the west coasts of Baranof and Chichagof. Such beds are prime sea otter habitat and provide protection, spawning habitat and food for a rich variety of marine life. (Stephen E. Hilson)

Above — The shallow pools at Bertha Bay on the west coast of Chichagof Island are warmed by White Sulphur Springs. (Ernest Manewal)

The ocean is rich in colorful sea life. At left, a tide pool abounds with common starfish. The octopus, center photo, is a common inhabitant of the outer tidelands, and is occasionally left in the seaweed when the tide goes out. At far right, three species of crab are found in the waters off Baranof and Chichagof islands: (clockwise from top) king, Dungeness, and tanner. All three have been harvested commercially. (left, R.E. Johnson; center and right, Loyal Johnson)

40

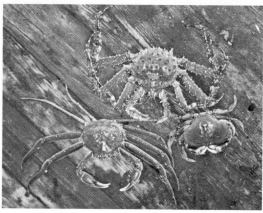

Above — Close examination of tide pools will reveal barnacles, mussels, limpets and hermit crabs (hidden in many different shells) in the seaweed. (Stephen E. Hilson)

Far left — Severe storms often batter the islands' coastlines, as shown in this photo taken near Port Alexander, at the southern tip of Baranof Island. (Matt Donohoe)

Left — With an abundance of spruce and cedar as raw materials, the Natives of Southeast Alaska became highly skilled carvers, as reflected in this carving on display at Sitka National Historical Park. (Rick Furniss, reprinted from *ALASKA GEOGRAPHIC®*)

The first Alaskans who came to Baranof and Chichagof islands moved over land which linked the northern continents where the waters of the Bering Sea now flow. For hundreds of years these hunters and their descendants journeyed along the coastline.

Although few evidences of these prehistoric cultures have been found in Southeast Alaska, a small bay on the northeast coast of Baranof Island, now called Kasnyku Bay or Hidden Falls, has yielded relics of these early people. The site of their early camp or village was exposed during construction of an Alaska Department of Fish & Game salmon hatchery. The U.S. Forest Service excavated the archaeological site in 1978-1979, and found evidence of three different periods of occupation.

Geological interpretation and radiocarbon dates from spruce wood fragments obtained from glacial deposits indicate that people were living at Hidden Falls before 9,800 years ago and perhaps as long as 11,000 years ago. Remains of a fire hearth and a few stone tools were found. Then sometime around 10,000 years ago, a small glacier flowed out of the mountains and over the Hidden Falls site covering it with 40 to 60 feet of ice.

When the glacier finally retreated, another group of people made their home at the exact location of the previous occupation without knowing that the stone tool remains of the earlier people lay beneath their feet. This occupation existed approximately 3,700 to 4,000 years ago. The people developed what archaeologists call a ground stone industry; scientists uncovered knives and points, ground stone adzes, mauls, drills, labrets, bone points, harpoons and awls.

For unknown reasons these people left and for a time the forest reclaimed the site. People again returned to the same place approximately 3,500 years ago, making the site their home until about 1,300 years ago.

These people had a tool tradition similar to the preceding occupation except for the addition of ground jade tools such as chisels, drills and adzes. Jade is not found locally so the people of Hidden Falls must have traded with other people — perhaps in British Columbia, the nearest known source of jade. Canoes undoubtedly provided transportation, and perhaps these people traveled considerable distances. The early inhabitants lived a marine-oriented existence and depended heavily on the ocean for subsistence. No hunting tools for mammals were found. The people of these last two occupations were typical of the Northwest Coast culture, but there is nothing at this point to identify them with the Tlingit culture.

This is only a tantalizing glimpse of the prehistory of the area around Sitka. Evidence of other such cultures which thrived on Baranof and Chichagof islands prior to the arrival of the Tlingits may someday be uncovered.

The recorded history of Sitka and the surrounding islands started in the mid-18th century, a time of Tlingit, Russian, Spanish, English, French and American adventurers. The first recorded sighting of what has been assumed to be Sitka Sound was made in 1741 during Vitus Bering's famous voyages leading to the discovery of what was to become Alaska. The *St. Paul*, under command of Alexei Chirikof, stood into a broad harbor at 57°15′ after crossing 3,000 miles of the unknown Pacific. A longboat was sent ashore to explore this new land. Days passed and no word or signal came. The remaining boat was sent to recall the party, but this boat too disappeared among the green islands. Smoke from fires within the bay could be seen from the ship, but three weeks passed and nothing was seen of the missing men. Some Natives in canoes paddled out from shore and after a rapid survey, returned to shore shouting in a language unknown to the Russians. Chirikof had no other boats to send in search of the Russian sailors, and he sadly set his course for the far shores of home. For more than 70 years the Russian government sought some sign of the sailors' fate, but their disappearance remains one of the unsolved mysteries of the northland.

Once the great land became more than a blank spot on a map, other navigators from many different countries set sail to explore the northwest coast. Possibly the next to see the Baranof Island coastline was Don Francisco de la Bodega y Quadra, one of the greatest Spanish navigators in the north. After many thrilling adventures and hardships, he sailed his 36-foot schooner *Sonora* into a broad bay (now known as Krestof Bay) which he called Port Guadalupe. The anchor was dropped on August 16, 1775.

Quadra wrote of a mountain "of the most regular and beautiful form I have ever seen." His name for the mountain, San Jacinto, was supplanted by the name given by Capt. James Cook in his third voyage of exploration in 1778. The beautiful cone today is known by the title Cook bestowed — Mount Edgecumbe. The Russians called the mountain Saint Lazaria, assuming the peak was the one seen by Chirikof and so named by him. The small island to the south is still known as Saint Lazaria Island.

It was Cook who brought to the attention of the civilized world the wealth of sea otter pelts available along the northwest coast. Because

Archaeological excavation at Hidden Falls, on the northeast coast of Baranof Island, has yielded evidence of a prehistoric camp. This ground slate tool, estimated to be thousands of years old, was unearthed at the site.
(Ricky Lightfoot)

Right — Archaeologists dig at Hidden Falls, recording the remains of prehistoric inhabitants who made their home there 4,000 years ago.
(U.S. Forest Service)

of its extraordinarily glossy and fluffy pelt, the sea otter was much prized by the Chinese upper class. The coat is dense, with thick, soft underfur and long guard hairs. The kelp and shellfish beds of the rocky and shallow coastal waters were teeming with these furbearers. Among the Natives of the coastal area, sea otters symbolized wealth and prestige.

It was because of the sea otter that Natives of the islands surrounding Sitka Sound came into contact with the European people and their culture. These people were Tlingits, the most northerly of the northcoast Indian nations. Here in Sitka Sound they maintained a permanent winter village. In the summer they led a nomadic life, scattering according to clan and family line to hunting and fishing territories. They undertook voyages to trade with neighboring Tlingits, such as the Hoonahs who lived in Port Frederick on Chichagof Island and who hunted and fished along Icy Strait.

Blueberries and red and blue huckleberries were picked at the forest's edge; clams were dug and crabs gathered from the tidal flats. The men hunted deer, brown bear and various birds. Herring eggs were collected by placing hemlock boughs in the ocean at herring spawning time.

Fish remained the main staple. Salmon were hooked or trapped in rock weirs; black cod and halibut were caught by lines. Herring, so plentiful in Sitka Sound, were raked into dugout canoes. With the approach of winter, the Tlingits reassembled in their village which they called "shee."

Long before the Europeans arrived, the Natives of Sitka and Southeast Alaska, stimulated by the temperate climate and lush flora and fauna, had a high degree of social stability and aesthetic creativity.

Identification with nature and interdepen-

dence with the environment around them was important to the Tlingits. They developed a system of beliefs based upon kinship and communication with all living things. The eagle and the raven became symbolic clan identifications. Various other symbols and art forms were developed.

The Natives impressed 18th century explorers with their skill in carving cedar and spruce. Ceremonial masks, rattles, dance paddles, everyday utensils all showed intricate designs of the eagle, raven, bear and other symbols. Sitka Tlingits decorated their homes only with house painting. Some mortuary columns rose near the gravehouses on the ridge back of the village, but great totem poles, which have come to be almost synonymous with the Northwest Coast Indians, were not part of the Sitka Tlingit's heritage.

The seeming boundless wealth of the Tlingits contributed to one of their most legendary customs, the potlach, which represented many things to Tlingit society: competition, confirmation of status, celebration and stimulation for the arts. Many occasions prompted a potlatch: honoring a dead chief, marriage, presentation of an heir, conferring of crests and rights. But always, the basic reason was to maintain prestige. This custom of potlatch was particularly important during the years when fur trading brought new and vast wealth to the chiefs or clan leaders who could give a potlatch.

It did not take long for the Natives to find that the men on the great sailing ships wanted sea otter pelts and were willing to trade a wide variety of goods for them. Once the Tlingits' desire for material goods was whetted by such popular trade items as Russian iron goods, Hudson's Bay Company blankets and American fabrics, foods and decorative items, their acquisitive nature increased.

More and more of the adventuresome navigators sailed their vessels to what was known as Sitka Sound or Norfolk Sound. By 1799 this part of the northwest coast was a favored trading spot. The Russians in their colony on Kodiak Island were jealous of the intruders on what they considered Russian domain.

There is no place in Southeast Alaska where the dual cultural heritage — Native and Russian — is more evident than at Sitka.

Left — An old Russian cannon still remains on Castle Hill, the site of the luxurious residence of Alexander Baranov, who established the first Russian settlement near Sitka. Baranov's house is pictured by artist Vasilly Ushanof on page 52. Castle Hill is also the site of the official transfer of Alaska to the United States by Russia in 1867.
(Dave Johnson)

Left inset — Native poles stand amid the cedar and spruce trees along the Indian River Trail at Sitka National Historical Park. Totem poles have become almost synonymous with the Northwest Coast Indians, and the collection at the park (primarily from Prince of Wales Island) is one of the finest. The Sitka Tlingits themselves did not carve poles, but their ceremonial masks, rattles, dance paddles and everyday utensils were carved in the same traditional designs.
(Matt Donohoe)

Right inset — The double-headed eagle in this detail from a Russian cannon at Sheldon Jackson Museum was a czarist crest.
(Ernest Manewal)

49

After a visit to the Sitka Sound area in 1795, Alexander Baranov, Chief Manager of the Russian-American Company, determined to build a company trading post and redoubt. On July 7, 1799 Baranov and his Aleut hunters arrived in Sitka Sound, purchased a tract of land from the local Tlingit chief and began construction of Saint Michael's Redoubt, six miles north of the present city. The hunters worked the passages between the islands, and sea otter skins were taken by the thousands.

The local Natives were divided among themselves in their feelings toward the new settlers. Some were friendly, while others viewed the intruders with great hostility. This came to a crisis in June 1802 when Natives attacked Saint Michael's Redoubt, burning and looting the barracks, storehouses and fur warehouses. A few Aleuts who had been hunting escaped to the English and American trading ships which had been anchored in the harbor at the time. These men bore the news of the tragedy to Baranov who had been away at Kodiak.

Two years passed before much is again known of Sitka. It is doubtful English and American captains dared to sail their ships into the harbor to gather furs. Then in 1804 Baranov returned to reestablish the redoubt, bringing a Russian warship, the *Neva*. The Native village was almost in the same place as the present town, grouped around what came to be known as Baranov's Hill. When Baranov's ships sailed into sight, the Natives abandoned the village in favor of a stronger fortification to the south by Indian River. After Baranov ordered the Russian ships stationed opposite the village, the *Neva* bombarded the Native encampment with 16 guns. A battle ensued at Indian River in which Baranov led the Russian forces. A few men were killed and some wounded including Baranov. Bombard-

continued on page 55

By 1806, the Russians had become more or less permanently established in Southeast Alaska. The fortified city of Sitka protected its Russian inhabitants from attacks by Tlingit warriors, which continued sporadically through the early part of the 19th century. (Courtesy of R.N. De Armond)

These two drawings, by an unknown artist, show Sitka as it was around 1825. The drawing on the right shows the original Saint Michael's Church, built close to the water in 1816. The church served until 1849, when the new Saint Michael's Cathedral was built. The drawing on the far right shows a view of the headquarters of the Russian-American Company. The fortified buildings were erected by Baranov in 1805; they were replaced by the Governor's House in 1837. (Both courtesy of R.N. De Armond)

50

51

Reconstructing Old Sitka on Canvas

Paintings by Vasilly V. Ushanoff, photos courtesy of the artist

At the age of 72, Dr. Vasilly Ushanoff, a retired dentist, became a self-taught painter. His brother-in-law, Alexander Doll, was a student of Russian-American history and got Dr. Ushanoff interested in painting that subject matter. After finding out that no sketches of the first Russian settlements at Sitka existed, Dr. Ushanoff set about re-creating the scenes on canvas, using written descriptions rather than illustrations. Ten months of research went into his painting of the Redoubt Saint Archangel Michael as it was in 1802.

Right — Redoubt Saint Archangel Michael, established in 1799 by Alexander Baranov, housed the first Russian settlers in Southeast Alaska, as well as a number of Aleuts brought in to hunt sea otters for the Russian-American Company. The large structure in the center of the painting was a warehouse; directly above it stood Baranov's house. Along the right side are, from the top: the stockade and blockhouse; the main building, with storage on the ground floor and living quarters above; the watchtower; and the *kashim*, or men's house, which served as a meeting place and steam room for the Aleut men. The entire settlement, along with the ship under construction in the foreground, was wiped out by Tlingit Indians in June, 1802. (Reprinted from *The ALASKA JOURNAL®*)

Above — After the Tlingit attack on the Redoubt Saint Archangel Michael, the settlement was never rebuilt on the same site. Baranov's new village, called New Archangelsk, was generally referred to as Sitka. This painting shows the town in 1806, with the newly designed flag of the Russian-American Company flying over Baranov's house.

This portrait shows Toion Kotlean, a Tlingit chief who was probably the leader of the attack on Old Sitka in 1802. When Baranov was recalled from his governorship of Alaska, the Indian came to bid him farewell prior to his departure, in November, 1818. According to K.T. Khlebnikov, whose biography of Baranov is the only one written from firsthand knowledge, Baranov had a great deal of respect for Toion Kotlean because of his intelligence and bravery.

53

Right — This steel engraving shows Sitka in 1837, with the newly completed Governor's House atop what is now known as Castle Hill. The engraving was made to accompany the narrative account of the voyage of the *Sulphur,* a ship which visited Sitka in September, 1837.

ment continued for several days until the Natives chose to abandon the fort and flee across the mountains to the north.

The Russians then began restoration of the post (officially named *Nova Arkhangelsk*, or New Archangel), this time on the present site of Sitka. A high, wooden stockade with three blockhouses, all armed with guns or cannons, was built around the hill overlooking the harbor. Within the stockade, warehouses, barracks and workshops began to take shape. Some were two stories high. Sitka was on its way to becoming the center of the Russian fur trade. Beginning in August 1808 New Archangel became the capital city of the Russian-American Company and the administrative center of the Russian colony.

Near the walls of the redoubt was the *ranche* where Sitka Natives returned in 1821 to occupy the site of their old village. The *Kolosh*, as the Natives were often called in those days, for the most part hunted and fished, lived in their tribal houses, carved their canoes and wove their baskets while residents within the fort gathered and prepared furs for shipping.

Warehouses were stored with thousands upon thousands of the richest furs of the north: sea otter, seal, land otter, marten, fox, mink, ermine, muskrat, beaver — pile after pile gathered from all over Russian America.

Sailing ships moved in and out of the harbor, taken to moorings or out to sea by the harbor tug. These ships brought supplies for inhabitants of the flourishing town. Some brought visitors and competing fur traders who wanted to see for themselves this metropolis in the wilderness. Others brought furs from outlying areas. Still other ships loaded the valuable furs for shipment to markets across the ocean. Ships came from the Yukon and other northern points; others were

Below — Alexander Baranov, first governor of Russian America, was a shrewd businessman and experienced manager. After building the first headquarters of the company at Kodiak in 1792, he moved it to Sitka in 1799 or 1800. Baranov's term as governor lasted from 1790 to 1818. (Courtesy of R.N. De Armond)

Left — As capital of Russian America, Sitka was known as New Archangel. It was the cultural and commercial center for an empire that stretched along the coast from Norton Sound all the way to California. This sketch probably dates from the 1850s or early 1860s. (Courtesy of R.N. De Armond)

en route to California or the Sandwich (Hawaiian) Islands. Still others were bound for the Kurile Islands, Okhotsk in Siberia or Canton in China.

Many of the captains of ships inbound for Sitka searched the rugged shoreline for a glimpse of light. For here, on top of the hill in the manager's residence, a light burned as a beacon to mariners entering the harbor, the first lighthouse to throw its beams over the turbulent waters of this northern sea.

Not all ships successfully navigated the uncharted waters. Perhaps best publicized of the shipwrecks along the coastline near Sitka was that of the *Neva* in 1813. Inbound from Okhotsk, the ship was plagued by storms the entire trip. Although Mount Edgecumbe was sighted, a storm drove the ship to sea where she beat about for weeks before again nearing port. In trying to make the harbor, the ship grounded on the rocks and broke to pieces under the terrific pounding of the waves. Some of the crew reached the shore. Two sailors went for help and persuaded a Native boy to take them to Sitka. Boats were fitted out and the survivors brought to Sitka. Thirty-eight perished, and the cargo of food and clothing, messages for the past year and rich vestments and furnishings for the church soon to be built in Sitka were scattered along the wild coast of Kruzof Island. Even today there are attempts to locate the wreck of the *Neva.*

Loss of the *Neva* delayed building of the Russian Orthodox Church. However, remnants of the rich collection of church articles were salvaged. According to Baranov, "the icon of Saint Michael outshone . . . all" of the other salvaged objects. Thus, when a small chapel was built in 1816, it was dedicated to Saint Michael. The eucharistic vessels for the church were made in Sitka from Spanish silver and the priest's vestments were fashioned

Opposite — This replica of a Russian blockhouse is similar to the one that once formed part of the stockade separating the Russian and Native sections of Sitka. (Stephen E. Hilson)

Below — This photo of the interior of the Governor's House was probably taken soon after the transfer of Alaska to the United States in 1867, before the structure was stripped of its furnishings. Visitors were always welcome at the residence, and Russian hospitality was world famous. The residence dominated Sitka's waterfront until it burned in 1894. (The Photo Shop, Sitka, courtesy of Richard A. Pierce)

oonah Natives in dance costume

from materials traded in China. After 25 years of use, the chapel deteriorated. With the aid of the Russian-American Company, a new church, Saint Michael's Cathedral, was built in the center of town. The cornerstone was laid in 1844, and the church was dedicated November 20, 1848.

By the time of the new cathedral, Sitka was in its golden age. The fur trade was still prosperous. Industries flourished in the capital city. Mechanics and artisans plied their trades. A shipyard had been established soon after the city was founded, and many vessels were built in the yard, including, in 1841, the first steam vessel to be constructed on the North Pacific, the *Politkofsky*. In addition, many vessels plying the northwest coast were repaired in Sitka.

Two sawmills supplied demands for lumber for ships and buildings. These buildings, it was found, lasted no longer than 20 years and often only 10 years partly because of the wet climate and partly because of fire.

Brickyards, tanneries and a foundry for casting brass, copper and iron were maintained. Native laborers, using a special saw, broke and sawed ice from the lakes. At times this ice was shipped to California. Swan Lake, known to the Russians as Labaishia Lake, was reported to have been created from a low swamp to provide this winter harvest of ice.

The Russians also built and maintained an outpost called Ozyorsk Redoubt at what is today the mouth of Redoubt Lake south of Sitka. The outpost consisted of a stockade, barracks, office, storehouse and barns.

Left and above — Saint Michael's Cathedral is the most impressive reminder of the part Russia played in Sitka's past. Although the original structure, built in 1849, was destroyed by fire in 1966, an exact copy was rebuilt on the same site from the original plans. (Stephen E. Hilson)

Right — A view of the interior of the new cathedral, where regular Russian Orthodox services are held. (Bob and Ira Spring)

Except for one large painting, some church records, and the church bells, everything of value was saved from Saint Michael's Cathedral during the 1966 fire. (Frank Roppel)

Because a good source of water power was nearby, Ozyorsk Redoubt was principally a manufacturing site. A water mill ground grain into flour and a tannery dressed the hides brought from California into shoe and other leather. A quarry for milling stones was found in the vicinity. Salmon were taken from the river and salted or dried for food.

At Sitka the Russians kept pigs, chickens and cows; hay was cut on the flats in nearby bays. Gardens of potatoes, turnips, lettuce and cabbage were cultivated. Yet food was not always plentiful. Keeping food at the remote capital was not easy and was always costly. Grain, purchased from California, Chile or from the Hudson's Bay Company, was ground into flour. Staples consisted of flour and fresh,

dried or salted fish. Deer, grouse and halibut were often the only fresh food in the capital some winters. The Russian-American Company labored long and hard, often with only fair success, to supply the food needs for Sitka.

Officers and employees of the Russian-American Company brought their families, and the citizens of Sitka lived a busy and often uneventful life. Usually only the arrival of ships, their departure and some great church festival disturbed the normal routine.

Easter was one of the greatest of the holidays. Most of the populace dressed in their finest apparel, attended services at church, then walked through town carrying gilded eggs to present to their friends.

The chief manager of the Russian-American

Company lived in the mansion on the hill overlooking the harbor. This residence was known as Baranov's Castle by the Americans although Baranov never saw the rectangular wood structure which dominated Sitka's waterfront until it burned in 1894.

At the manager's table sat the captain of the port, the secretaries and others of high station in the colony. Visitors were welcomed, and Russian hospitality was world famous.

For the majority of inhabitants amusements were few and simple: boating and quiet rambles along the road known as the Governor's Walk to the deep woods near Indian River. Socializing was the townspeople's favorite pastime.

By the mid-1800s Russia's interest in her New World colony waned. Company profits were only fair. The Crimean War had revealed the colony's vulnerability to seaborne conquerors. The Russian-American Company and Hudson's Bay Company had made a peace pact during the war. A combined British-French fleet, which had bombarded and destroyed Petropavlovsk on the Siberian coast, sailed across the Pacific to Sitka to make sure the town was remaining neutral and was not harboring any warships. The British and French found no enemy warships and signaled the Russians onshore that they meant no harm.

But these and other facts convinced the Russians that the wisest move was to sell the remote colony. The United States was the logical purchaser. A purchase treaty was signed by Secretary of State William Henry Seward on March 29, 1867, and was ratified by Congress on June 20, 1867. Alaska was formally turned over to the United States in Sitka on October 18, 1867 for a purchase price of $7.2 million. Thus began a new era for the town of Sitka.

Above — Among the church icons is a relic from Saint Herman (left), first Russian Orthodox saint in the United States. (Bob and Ira Spring)

Left — Cast in Russia, the original bronze bells of Saint Michael's melted in the fire that destroyed the church in 1966. They were recast to duplicate the originals when the church was rebuilt. (Ernest Robertson)

Clockwise from far left —

■ This engraving, made around 1885, shows the back of Saint Michael's Cathedral. The large building on the left was known as The Clubhouse, and originally housed single male employees of the Russian-American Company.

■ Three Russian-built log structures still stood in Sitka in the 1870s and 1880s. At the top of the engraving is the Governor's House, known as Baranov's Castle, which dominated the skyline until it was destroyed by fire in 1894. The building at the left was originally used as offices for the Russian-American Company, with a school on the second floor. It later became the U.S. Customs House and site of other government offices before it burned in 1936. The building at the right was used as a barracks by the Russians, and later by the U.S. Army and Marine Corps. It also housed a jail, and was eventually torn down around 1920.

■ This drawing of Sitka, one of the first made following the United States' purchase of Alaska, shows the American flag flying high above the Governor's House. The drawing was done between 1867 and 1869.

(Alaska Division of Tourism)

64

Above and left — Some of the oldest names in Sitka's history are carved on the crumbling grave markers of its many cemeteries. (Above, Tim Thompson; left, Ernest Robertson)

Left — The first resident of the Russian Bishop's House was Bishop Innocent, who took up residence there in 1843. The far left photo, taken by an unknown passenger aboard the S.S. *Ancon* in the summer of 1885, shows the house to be somewhat dilapidated. The shedlike structures at either end of the building were removed in later years and replaced by additions to the building, as can be seen in the left photo, taken in 1976. Today the house is one of the oldest standing wooden structure in Alaska, and is in the process of being restored as part of the Sitka National Historical Park. (Far left, courtesy of R.N. De Armond; left, Patricia Roppel)

Sitka's profile in 1867 showed several large log buildings: the governor's residence, hospital, barracks, warehouses and the faded, blue-gray Saint Michael's Cathedral. The stockade dividing the town from the *ranche,* the Native quarter, was dilapidated. Once this barricade had represented the difference between life and death during the years after Baranov's reconquest of Sitka. But not since 1855 had Sitka Natives attacked the fort. Within the Native village the old communal structures had been torn down and replaced with frame buildings.

Fur trading continued on a small scale. Independent traders collected furs, and in 1870 estimates attributed two-thirds of Southeast Alaska's fur trade to the Sitka area.

During the first years after purchase, the U.S. Army became the official peacemaker between Natives and adventurers who arrived after the majority of Russians left for home. Orders for the Army's withdrawal came in 1877, and the village was left in the hands of United States Customs officials.

One week after the Army's departure, Sitka's segregated Natives tore down a portion of the stockade and it was never rebuilt. Again in February 1879, fear of an Indian uprising swept Sitka. Both the Natives and the prospectors, with time on their hands, were frequently drunk. Street fights and random killings resulted. Before matters quieted down an English warship, the H.M.S. *Osprey,* was called in. Whether or not there was imminent danger, the *Osprey* affair was humiliating. Soon after, the U.S. Navy was given the task of maintaining law and order in the district.

This lasted until 1884 when John H. Kinkead became Alaska's first governor appointed by a United States President, and Sitka became the seat of the first form of Alaska civilian government.

This 1890 painting depicts the Sitka Industrial and Training School, now known as Sheldon Jackson College. The campus included, from left: separate boys' and girls' dormitories; a church; Elliott F. Shepard Hall; a museum (behind the hall); a girls' hospital; several cottages; and a boys' hospital. (Tongass Historical Society Museum)

About this time Alaska's oldest educational institution, Sitka Industrial and Training School (now known as Sheldon Jackson College), was founded. In 1878 mission work was started by J.G. Brady, who was sent by the Board of Home Missions. A year later A.E. Austin began teaching a day school in Sitka. Then in 1881 the first building on the present college site was erected under the direction of Reverend Sheldon Jackson of the Board of National Missions of the United Presbyterian Church. Sitka Industrial and Training School became an institution which taught Native students regular classroom subjects and trades such as carpentry and shipbuilding. The school was partially funded by the govern-

ment, and was operated by the Board of Missions.

More buildings were constructed, and by 1911 the facility was known as Sheldon Jackson School. The institution met the changing educational needs of Native Alaskans through a series of boarding schools beginning with vocational training, an elementary school and a high school. Today Sheldon Jackson is an accredited two-year college.

By the mid-1890s Sitka, Alaska's capital, reflected a typical late 19th century American hamlet with churches, a hospital, mercantile stores, schools, a newspaper office and a free reading room and library.

One of the churches was Saint Peter's-by-the-Sea, an Episcopal church which today stands overlooking Crescent Harbor. The church was built in 1899 chiefly because of the influence of Peter Trimble Rowe, first Episcopal bishop of Alaska. A woman from New York whose husband had visited Sitka in 1897 provided funds for the distinctive building of stone and wood. Bishop Rowe, who came to Sitka in 1896, and his first wife are buried in the churchyard.

Sitka remained the capital until 1900 when it was transferred to booming Juneau. In 1904 the port of entry in the Customs collection district was moved from Sitka to Juneau, making Sitka a subport. After the capital actually moved in 1906, Sitka became a quiet village.

During this transition period, in 1901, Sitka became the base station of a magnetic observatory. The Coast and Geodetic Survey had received complaints from mariners about local deflection of the compass which they encountered in various places in Alaska. Some compass disturbances were so great they caused ships to go aground.

Sitka Industrial and Training School taught Native students regular academic subjects as well as useful arts such as carpentry and shipbuilding. The school was financed by the government and was operated by the Presbyterian Board of Missions. Here, a class of young men pose with their teacher in front of a partially completed boat in 1907. (Tongass Historical Society Museum)

A site above the Native village was determined to have the least local disturbance, and magnetic variation instruments were installed. In 1903 seismographic equipment was added. Known as the Sitka Magnetic and Seismological Observatory, the facility obtained basic magnetic data for the control of magnetic surveys. The town's growth and subsequent steel and iron construction required moving the delicate instruments to the present site above the National Cemetery in 1940.

The National Cemetery, with the oldest

69

burial date of December 1867, also contains the graves of early members of the American forces in the occupation of Alaska. After years of neglect, Alaska's governor, Scott C. Bone, urged the graveyard's designation as a National Cemetery. President Calvin Coolidge complied in 1924, making the Sitka cemetery the only national graveyard west of the Rocky Mountains until World War II.

Another permanent contribution to Sitka begun prior to World War I was the establishment by the First Territorial Legislature in 1913 of a Pioneers' Home for indigent prospectors who had spent many years in Alaska. At the request of the legislature, the U.S. Navy granted permission for use of the abandoned barracks buildings.

Although in disrepair and inadequate for its purpose, the old barracks remained in use until March 1934 when 170 men moved into the present main building of the Pioneers' Home. Not until 1956 was a long-cherished dream realized when women pioneers moved into a new wing of the home.

The 13½-foot-tall bronze statue of The Prospector in front of the Pioneers' Home was not unveiled until 1949, culminating nearly 20 years of effort and planning. Victor Alonzo Lewis, a sculptor in Seattle, created a model of the Argonaut of the North modeled after a true pioneer, William "Skagway Bill" Fonda. The statue is a composite, however, of an army of men, invincible pioneers whom nothing could stop.

With World War II Sitka began to boom. Japonski Island, across the channel from Sitka, had been a naval reserve since the 1890s and became a full-scale navy air base, complete with ammunition dumps and several large seaplane hangers. There was talk for a time of making Japonski a submarine base.

Saint Peter's-by-the-Sea, consecrated on Easter Sunday, 1900, still stands today overlooking Crescent Harbor. The church was built by Peter Trimble Rowe, the first Episcopal bishop of Alaska. The bishop and his wife are buried in the churchyard. (Frank Shoemaker)

Left — These two photos, taken from Mount Verstovia looking west, show the dramatic changes which took place in Sitka between 1939 (top) and 1961 (bottom). (Top, Rolphe Dauphin, R.N. De Armond Collection; bottom, The Photo Shop Studio)

At Sitka National Cemetery the oldest burial date is December, 1867, nine months after the treaty to purchase Alaska was signed. Designated a National Cemetery in 1924, it was the only such graveyard west of the Rocky Mountains until World War II. (Shelley Schneider)

A radio "beam" station was constructed on Biorka Island on the south side of Sitka Sound. The U.S. Army built a base on adjacent islands, naming the base Fort Ray after Lieutenant P.K. Ray of the 8th Infantry who had been in charge of registering food supplies for the thousands of gold seekers coming into the territory in 1897. In addition, there were gun emplacements on Harbor Peak and on several islands in Sitka Sound.

Sitka sprang to life during this period. New stores, improved telephone system, new bank, a hotel and new homes were built for the influx of workers. During this time residents of Sitka lived with brownouts and blackouts and constant vigils for signs of the enemy.

With armistice, the facilities on Japonski Island were placed in the hands of the Department of Interior for use as a medical and educational facility. In 1955 the hospital was

The approach to Sitka by air is often startling to first-time visitors, as the runway seems to disappear into the ocean.
(Betty Johannsen)

placed under the U.S. Public Health Service. A boarding school, Mount Edgecumbe School, for Natives from throughout Alaska was begun by the Bureau of Indian Affairs and continues today, often under the threat of closure from lack of funds.

The Sitka airport was constructed on Japonski Island. The U.S. Coast Guard expanded its facilities here in 1977 to enforce the 200-mile limit regulations.

With these facilities on the island, a permanent link between Sitka and Japonski Island was urgently needed. A shoreboat crossed the channel at half-hour intervals, and on occasions the water was too rough for navigation. The shoreboat was novel, but readily lost its appeal when inconveniences were encountered. Thus 1,225-foot O'Connell Bridge, the first cable-stayed girder span bridge built in the United States, was dedicated in 1972.

All of these improvements and expansions have modernized the Sitka-of-old. However, Sitka continues to be the service center for development of natural resources on the land and in the sea.

The fur supply, once a rich heritage and prime stimulus for occupation and settlement in Alaska, diminished as the furbearers were exploited. During Russian occupation and for a few years after the purchase of Alaska, the fur industry was the only industry in Alaska. After discovery of gold and subsequent development of mining, fur became less and less a part of Southeast Alaska's economy. Today the fur industry's importance is rarely remembered.

73

For years, however, trade in land mammal furs was an important factor on Baranof and Chichagof islands. Fur buyers made annual visits on steamers going from place to place to gather furs. Trappers on these two islands had limited opportunity for trapping compared to the rest of Alaska. Only the brown bear, ermine, mink and land otter were indigenous to the islands while elsewhere in Alaska trappers could stalk black bear, marten, fisher, fox, lynx, beaver and wolf. These limitations resulted in introduction of marten and beaver to Baranof and Chichagof islands.

Until the 1930s, Sitka Native hunters participated in pelagic sealing close to the islands off Sitka Sound. They sought the northern fur seal herd on its annual migration northbound to the Pribilof Islands in the Bering Sea.

In 1903 Sitka Natives took more than 300 fur seal skins. Because so few fur seal hides were taken in the territory, these skins brought tremendous prices. By a fur seal treaty in 1911, Natives were restricted to use of spears and clubs — traditional methods of capture — instead of firearms.

Deer hides were also taken for a number of years around the early 1900s. Many Natives earned money harvesting deer and selling the hides at the closest store. Protests by miners and others dependent upon deer as a food staple soon led to a regulation prohibiting hunting of deer just for the hide. Today the Alaska Department of Fish and Game sets seasons and limits.

Lax laws for certain species of furbearers continued to represent inadequate protection and the annual output of furs decreased. Stringent regulations were enacted in the 1920s which allowed some furbearers to renew populations. Yet the world's fashion centers still sought furs for ornamentation, garments and lap robes.

Farming of furbearing animals seemed an answer. Successful and often lucrative propagation of furbearers, particularly the blue phase of the arctic fox, began in eastern Canada. Soon raising furbearers caught on in Alaska, especially near Kodiak and Afognak islands in the western Gulf of Alaska. The successful beginnings in Southeast Alaska were not in the Sitka area, but rather at Sumdum south of Juneau. The industry stumbled along until about 1920 by which time the techniques of culture had been pioneered. In addition to foxes, the farmers raised few marten and many mink.

Raising blue foxes in a semi-wild state where the animals were free to roam was strictly an Alaska idea, and pioneer fox farmers had many obstacles to overcome. Small islands, far enough from shore to discourage animals from escaping, were leased. Here the foxes hunted, and on some islands they were able to find sufficient food. On other islands there was so little prey that practically the entire food supply for the foxes had to be furnished from elsewhere.

Isolated fur farmers ingeniously scavenged food for their animals by keeping a skate or tow of halibut gear, a crab trap or two and nets in season. If a farmer was near a settlement, he often could acquire fish heads and scrap fish from the canneries and cold storages. The seafood diet could be varied with waste scraps from deer, with squirrels and mice, and supplemented with grains.

Many fur-farming operations near Sitka were inconspicuous and were overlooked in the earliest years of the industry. A Mr. Johnson raised mink and marten in Sitka in 1913. By 1919 fox farms were located on Hoonah Island in Icy Strait and on Hill Island off the west coast of Chichagof Island.

Islands off Chichagof and Baranof proved to

Clockwise from right —
■ Blue foxes feed at a farm on Biorka Island, probably in the 1920s. Many fox farms were established on the islands around Baranof and Chichagof in the early part of the century. The industry declined during the depression and never recovered. (Ann De Groat, Alaska Historical Library)
■ Four-year-old Jorgen Thomsen stands in front of the feed house at a fox farm on Biorka Island. The house was used for cooking cereal to supplement the foxes' diets. (Ann De Groat, Historical Library)
■ By establishing fox farms on small islands, far enough from shore to prevent the animals from escaping, the foxes could be raised in a semi-wild state, where they were free to roam and hunt. This farm owned by Chris Jackson was located on Legma Island (also called Legina Island), about three miles west of Goddard. (Ann De Groat, Alaska Historical Library)

be ideal for fox farming. These islands were small, close to Sitka where fish wastes could be obtained for food and were often endowed with a natural food supply. Small cabins and garden plots, home for the farmer and his family, soon appeared on islands such as Long, Galankin, Crow, Middle, Siginaka, Error, Berry and Big and Little Gavansky in Sitka Sound. Among the islands of the outer Baranof coast, foxes flourished on the Necker group, including Biorka, Gornoi, Elovoi, Legma, Maid, Tava, Taigud, Peiser and Kasiana. On Hogan and Hill islands off Chichagof, blue foxes roamed and multiplied.

Using Hoonah as a supply center, fox farmers collected the prime pelts each January on George, Inian and Halibut islands. Hoonah Fox Farms operated on Hoonah Island. Klokachef Island on the north side of Salisbury Sound, Porcupine Island at the south end of Lisianski Strait and Three Hill Island just west of Elfin Cove all had foxes. Cedar Island and Redcliff Islands in Freshwater Bay supported fox farms.

Many fox farms lasted only a year or so. Some fox farmers combined moonshining with fox farming, with perhaps more emphasis on the former. There was a good market for moonshine with two mines and a number of prospects on west Chichagof, and fox farming made a good blind. Many farmers fed their foxes a mixture of fish and grain so the moonshiners had an excuse for buying corn and barley.

Then came the Great Depression, and fox farming dropped to a low level. The industry never recovered. One by one the islands and the foxes were abandoned. Most of the animals were poached and sold for minimal prices. Others could not survive without the supplemental food supply. Island fox farming is now a thing of the past.

Today commercial trapping seasons and bag limits are regulated primarily by abundance and market values. Closures cover the breeding period and the time when the fur is not prime.

Fluctuating pelt prices, increased levels of other types of employment and the availability of public assistance programs have resulted in reduced trapping. Few full-time professional trappers remain, but some people continue to trap to supplement their incomes. Mink, native to Baranof and Chichagof, and marten, introduced to the two islands, continue to be trapped and sold commercially. Short-tailed weasels or ermines are no longer of major importance and are usually taken incidental to trapping of other furbearers. Most furs are still sold to buyers from the Lower 48 states.

L ike their predecessors, such as the people at Hidden Falls, the Tlingits derived their principal nourishment from the sea. Salmon were taken in traps, with hooks or by spears. Much was dried for winter food. Halibut were consumed both fresh and smoked.

Herring were found in the spring along the coast and inner channels and were dipped out with nets or baskets, caught with drag nets or taken with rakes. Herring roe constituted an important food. Herring deposited millions of eggs upon hemlock boughs, fastened on the beach at low tide. The egg-laden branches were collected again and hung to dry. One early writer described the drying process as "giving an appearance not unlike a heavy fall of snow upon the trees."

Like the Tlingits, the Russians sought the

Right — Fishing has long been a mainstay of Sitka's economy. Long hours of trolling keep the fish boxes full. (Chip Porter)

Top inset — Scott Landis works the gear on his 35-foot troller patroling Chatham Strait for salmon. (Tom Paul)

Bottom inset — A fisherman weighs his catch of red snapper. (Matt Donohoe)

salmon. At Sitka the supply of salmon was largely procured from Ozyorsk Redoubt, approximately 16 miles to the southwest. Here in the rocky wall which divides Redoubt Lake from the sea and over which the lake's outlet flowed, channels were blasted for reservoirs. In these channels the Russians placed *zapors,* or fences, which formed traps into which the salmon swam and lay in cool, clear ponds until they were removed for use. The Russians also preserved salt salmon for winter use. From 300 to 500 barrels were salted each year.

The salmon resource did not come into its own until 20 years after Alaska's purchase. The sheer numbers of fish made it inevitable that this natural treasure would be exploited on an increasing scale. In 1878 the founding of two small canneries, one at Klawock on Prince of Wales Island and the other at Sitka initiated

what would soon become one of the major pillars of the territory's economy.

Cutting and Company of San Francisco began construction late in the season on a cannery at what is called "Old Sitka," near the site Baranov first built his redoubt. Somehow crews succeeded in hammering together a structure, installing machinery, and preparing cans and shipping boxes in time to process some of the 1878 catch.

The next year Cutting and Company experienced a near riot caused by importation of Chinese laborers from San Francisco. The Sitka Natives wanted to fish and do the canning. One chief was reported to have informed the Cutting superintendent, "If an Indian can make a hoochinoo still, he can make a can to hold salmon." The infuriated Natives were pacified only after they were

Left — A large salmon cannery was located on Sitkoh Bay, on the southeast tip of Chichagof Island, shown here in 1914. The cannery was built by Peter and son August Buschmann in 1900 and later was taken over by Pacific Packing & Navigation Company. After that firm went bankrupt, the cannery was purchased in 1907 by George T. Myers, who operated it for many years. It finally closed in 1974 and was destroyed by fire in 1978. (Department of Commerce, U.S. Bureau of Fisheries)

Above — Boatloads of herring are delivered to Red Bluff Bay about 1925. The bay's existing salmon cannery was quickly converted in the early 1920s to the more profitable business of processing herring. The fish were abundant, and the industry was booming following a sharp rise in the price of herring oil. (Howard Wakefield, Patricia Roppel collection)

Left — A herring plant was built at Red Bluff Bay in 1922 by Wakefield Fisheries alongside the salmon cannery they purchased that year from Baranoff Packing Company. Both fish were packed there until 1925, when the facility was converted totally to processing herring. The plant, which burned in 1937, packed kippered and Scotch-cured herring, and produced herring oil and fish meal for fertilizer. (Howard Wakefield, Patricia Roppel collection)

Left — A plant located at Little Port Walter, shown here in 1920, was said to be the first cannery in Alaska to pack herring. Later a salmon and herring cannery, cold storage, and reduction plant producing both salmon and herring oil and fertilizer operated at Little Port Walter. The last salmon pack was made there in 1925. (Alaska Historical Library, reprinted from *The ALASKA JOURNAL®*)

The Port Armstrong shore station of the United States Whaling Company (left) began operating in 1912. Shown here in 1914, the plant processed the entire whale — oil from blubber, meat and bones, and reduction of residue into fertilizer. The photo below shows the carcass of a large sperm whale at the station after the blubber has been removed. (Top, Patricia Roppel collection; bottom, Department of Commerce, U.S. Bureau of Fisheries)

promised that the Chinese would come north only to instruct the Natives. This attitude did not prevail in Alaska for long, and the packing force in most canneries became predominately Chinese.

Labor troubles, marketing problems and financial difficulties caused the fledgling business to cease operation at the end of the second year. The Old Sitka cannery was dismantled, and the equipment shipped to Cook Inlet where the company began anew.

Salting salmon and packing them in barrels proved to be less labor intensive and cheaper. A few salteries began to pack salmon at Port Althorp and Sandy Bay.

Eleven years after the abandonment of Old Sitka cannery another attempt was made in the Sitka district to can salmon. Canneries began in 1889 at Pavlof Harbor on Chichagof Island and on Baranof Island at Redoubt Lake, the same site as that used by the Russians.

However, the outer coasts of Baranof and Chichagof were considered the most difficult to fish at that time. The streams all drained into unsurveyed bays, and sockeye runs were considered small and uncertain. The operation at Redoubt Lake lasted one year before it was moved to Redfish Bay, farther south on the outer coast.

Steamers plying the often stormy waters searched for fish in Little Whale Bay and Necker Bay on Baranof; Smith, Olsen and O'Hara bays on Chichagof; and Surge Bay on Yakobi. After eight years the Redfish Bay cannery closed. Except for the plant in Ford Arm on Chichagof Island, which lasted from 1912 to 1923, no other cannery sought a remote outer coastal site.

After the turn of the century, gas engines became common, and made fishing from a central location more economical. Sitka became the center of the outer coast fisheries.

Development of refrigeration facilities opened new markets, and by 1913 cold storage plants were opening throughout Southeast Alaska and at Prince Rupert, British Columbia. This development breathed new life into Sitka's fisheries. At the new cold storage of Booth Fisheries, opened in Sitka in 1913, a chain of vessels waited to take on ice. Clerks in the mercantile store busily assembled orders. The cold storage not only froze fish, but had refrigeration for holding tierces of mild-cured salmon. Mild-curing of chinook and coho salmon continued to be an active business for many years.

By 1919 Sitka's cold storage froze the second largest number of pounds of fish in Alaska. Sablefish (black cod), salmon and halibut were delivered to the docks. Halibut banks had been found within a 25-mile radius, and by 1912 one man boat catches of 25 to 100 fish a day were being made.

At various times Dungeness crab were processed. In one operation in 1922, crab were caught in traps, brought to the dock, butchered, the meat extracted by compressed air and the product canned. Several canneries

Top — The large facilities of the Hoonah Packing Company were built in 1912 about 2 miles from the village of Hoonah. Shown here in 1917, the plant continued to process salmon until 1944. The buildings are still standing today and are used by local fishermen to store their boats and nets. (Courtesy of Harold Brindle, reprinted from *ALASKA GEOGRAPHIC*®)

Above — This 1897 photo shows the Baranoff Packing Company Cannery at Redfish Bay, about 10 miles northwest of Port Alexander. The cannery opened in 1891 and could process 500 cases of salmon per day. It closed after eight years of operation. (Moser, *Salmon Fisheries of Alaska*, Plate 46, reprinted from *ALASKA GEOGRAPHIC*®)

Right — This dilapidated bunkhouse is all that remains today of the Chatham Straits Fish Company herring reduction plant at New Port Walter. (Patricia Roppel)

operated at Tenakee Springs. King crab from Icy Strait as well as Dungeness crab were processed for a time in the late 1930s at Hoonah.

Salmon canneries operated along Sitka's waterfront. After Cutting and Company left the Old Sitka site in 1880, no cannery ran there until 1917 when Sitka Packing Company began operations. The next year a rival, Pyramid Packing Company, started their processing equipment. After 1924 this facility was Sitka's only cannery for many years except for an occasional custom pack outfit which would last a year or two.

Meanwhile fishermen discovered runs of pink and chum salmon in the calmer inside waters off the eastern coast of Baranof and Chichagof. At remote sites on Chichagof Island, salmon were cleaned and cut into pieces to fill the cans. At Chatham on Sitkoh Bay, Todd on Peril Strait, Pavlof Harbor in Freshwater Bay, fishing boats, heavily laden with salmon, unloaded at the docks. At the Native village of Hoonah, and at the hot springs village of Tenakee Springs, residents found work processing the fish. The fishing communities of Pelican and Elfin Cove were in later years carved out of the wilderness of north Chichagof Island.

On the rugged southern tip of Baranof Island, at Port Alexander, up to a thousand fishing boats, mostly trollers, fished Cape Ommaney, Larch Bay and the outer shore of south Baranof Island.

In 1917 three canneries began to process salmon at Red Bluff Bay, Little Port Walter and Big Port Walter along Baranof's eastern shore. In 1920 a cannery opened at Port Conclusion. However, these salmon canneries were quickly converted in the early 1920s to the more lucrative business of processing abundant herring.

Opposite — Early morning mist touches the fishing fleet at Port Alexander. Formerly one of the busiest fishing ports in Southeast, the community almost died when the great runs of salmon vanished in the 1930s. Now a small but determined fleet works out of the port at the southern tip of Baranof Island. (Tom Paul)

Above — Because of a decline in the number of whales taken annually, the Port Armstrong shore station ceased processing the animals in 1923. The station was then leased for herring salting and reduction, and saw duty as a submarine base during World War II. By the time this photo was taken, around 1948, the plant was back to the business of reducing herring to oil and fertilizer. (Courtesy of National Marine Fisheries Service — Alaska, reprinted from *ALASKA*® magazine)

Right — In 1965, the last herring reduction plant in Southeast Alaska, located at Big Port Walter, ceased operation. The plant was later destroyed by fire. (Stephen E. Hilson)

The price of herring oil had risen by this time to such an extent that the industry was booming. After the oil was extracted, the meal was dried for fertilizer. Large herring were salted. Salted or pickled herring had long been a staple food in Europe and elsewhere, but Alaska herring, salted in barrels by various methods, never competed with herring packed in Scotland or Norway. Small herring predominated in south Chatham Strait, and these fish were unacceptable for pickling. All salting of herring was adjunct to the oil and fish meal business.

Each herring plant utilized fleets of four to six large seiners varying in size from 59 to 75 feet in length. These fished the rough waters of Chatham Strait, and then sought the calm waters of the deep bays. At Big Port Walter, Port Conclusion, Port Herbert, Little Port Walter, New Port Walter, Deep Cove, Warm Springs Bay and Red Bluff Bay, the shouts of the crews and the clank of machinery echoed for four months of the year. Then came silence, broken only by the sounds of the lone watchman.

By the 1940s the herring runs were declining, markets were going down hill and production of herring oil and fertilizer was greatly reduced. From that time on, adjustments were made yearly to protect herring populations. Catches of herring continued on a greatly reduced basis, and one by one the plants were closed. In 1965 the last, at Big Port Walter, ceased operation. Since that time no herring have been reduced to oil and fertilizer in this area.

Another fishery flourished for a brief time off Baranof Island. Steam whalers of the United States Whaling Company, which had a shore plant at Port Armstrong, intercepted the northward migration of whales. With its fleet, the *Star I*, *Star II*, and *Star III*, the company

sought blue, right, sperm, fin or finback and humpback whales, beginning in 1912. Workers at the shore plant processed the entire carcass: oil from blubber, meat and bones; and fertilizer from the residue. During the first year the fleet brought in an exceptional catch of 314 whales. The company confidently expanded facilities to handle 500 whales a season, but annual catches diminished.

By 1922 the company caught only 117 whales including 60 sperm whales, producing only 6,000 barrels of oil. Whales were taken only one more year, and the station was then leased for herring salting and reduction.

Another fishery boomed for an even briefer period. Shark fishing — part of the halibut and black cod fishery –– was carried on out of Sitka and Tenakee as well as many other Alaska ports. Fishermen began saving shark livers when they became valuable as a source of Vitamin A for the Armed Forces during World War II. The varnished, brass-looking, five-gallon cans filled with livers and lashed in the waist of halibut schooners were a common sight. Synthetics killed this side fishery after World War II.

Today the fisheries on Baranof and Chichagof islands are only a shadow compared to the past. Whaling was never renewed after 1923. The herring fishery has declined to a fraction of its former magnitude because of cheaper sources of fish meal and decreasing demand for herring products. Today herring are primarily harvested for bait and for sac-roe to be exported to Japan. The sac-roe herring fishery in Sitka Sound takes place in late spring when many seiners congregate to participate in a fishery which may be only open for a few hours. Management of this rich and controversial fishery calls for use of special acoustical sounding equipment to

Opposite — The crew of the *Atlas* brings the seine aboard during a set in Necker Bay, on the west coast of Baranof Island. (R.E. Johnson)

Left — A cold storage worker helps unload salmon from a troller at the dock at Sitka Sound Seafoods. (Matt Donohoe)

Below — Fishing boats gather around the cookhouse, oil dock, at Pelican, which has its own cold storage facility. (Chip Porter)

monitor herring stocks so that harvest levels are kept within acceptable limits.

A fairly large fishing fleet of seiners, power trollers and hand trollers still calls Sitka home. The outlook is sufficiently bright that the Halibut Producers Cooperative built a new cold storage there in 1980. This nonprofit organization, owned by American fishermen, processes salmon, black cod and herring in addition to halibut. This is the cooperative's first Alaska processing plant and it joins Sitka Sound Seafoods, which also processes fish and provides ice to the fishermen.

Above — Fishing vessels wait to unload fish at Sitka Sound Seafoods, one of two processors located at Sitka. (Patricia Roppel)

Fish buying stations are maintained in season at such remote harbors as Goddard on Baranof, Kalinin Bay on Kruzof, and Deer Harbor on Yakobi. Salmon caught by power trollers and hand trollers are iced by the men at the buying stations before shipment to Sitka, where the fish are prepared for freezing.

Processors also handle black cod or sablefish, Pacific and lingcod, halibut, red snapper and salmon of all species. Tanner, king and Dungeness crab are delivered to the cold storage plants. Occasional loads of shrimp which reach Sitka are sold dockside to local residents. Salmon eggs, which the fishermen save when cleaning fish aboard their boats, are sold and processed also, much of it, "golden caviar," for the Oriental market.

Cold storage plants dominate the waterfronts in Hoonah, Pelican and Port Alexander. Fish buying stations handle the catch at Tenakee and Elfin Cove.

Sport fishing also represents a considerable recreational and economic resource in the Sitka area. Steelhead, rainbow and cutthroat trout and Dolly Varden are taken by anglers fishing the fresh-water lakes and streams. Many sport fishermen troll Sitka Sound for salmon, while others cast from the beaches. Many additional salmon are taken in sport and subsistence fisheries around small villages and logging camps scattered throughout the region.

In recent years fishermen, state and federal agencies and others concerned with the diminishing runs of salmon decided to invest in the future by artificially producing more fish.

A National Marine Fisheries Service research station at Little Port Walter on southeast Baranof Island conducts research on natural salmon runs and salmon enhancement techniques. This information is available and used by the hatcheries to produce salmon for the common property fisheries.

In 1974 the state legislature approved a permit system whereby qualified nonprofit corporations could construct and operate salmon hatcheries. One of the first such hatcheries to begin operations, a facility at Sheldon Jackson College in Sitka, has enjoyed substantial returns of adult pink salmon since 1976.

Hatcheries are in the planning stage or are under construction on the Maksoutof River, which flows into Sandy Bay on Baranof Island's west coast, by the Tlingit and Haida Central Council; on Medvejie Lake, which drains into Silver Bay near Sitka, by the Northern Southeast Regional Aquaculture Association; and at Port Armstrong on southeast Baranof Island.

Above — Spotlessly clean after hours, the Pelican Cold Storage fish house awaits another day of deliveries. (Chip Porter)

Left — While salmon brought in the big dollars for fishermen on Baranof and Chichagof islands, herring also contributed substantially to their income. Herring was salted or pickled, or reduced to oil and fish meal. Ruins of this abandoned reduction plant (earlier the site of a whaling station for the U.S. Whaling Company) lined the shores of Port Armstrong, but in the past couple of years the buildings have been torn down and a private nonprofit salmon hatchery has been built on the site. (Tom Paul)

Right — When the weather turns foul, fishermen seek quiet harbors in which to wait out the storms on the fishing grounds. Here a troller anchors at the base of a waterfall in Mist Cove, on the southeast coast of Baranof Island. (Matt Donohoe)

Below — Research on chinook salmon enhancement techniques are conducted at a National Marine Fisheries Service research station at Little Port Walter. These chinook salmon returned after being released as fry from the station. They were spawned and the eggs will provide the basis for further research. (Patricia Roppel)

Northern Southeast Regional Aquaculture Association, the regional corporation which includes Baranof and Chichagof islands, represents commercial fishermen, seafood processors and interested persons who use the resource. Plans are to stock lakes on Kruzof and Baranof islands with coho salmon. This species requires at least one year in fresh water before migration to sea. Coho fry will spend their fresh-water rearing period in lakes which can support fish but do not normally have a coho run.

For a number of years the Alaska Department of Fish & Game operated an experimental facility to rear coho salmon in salt-water net pens at Starrigavan Creek. Today the department's attention is focused at Hidden Falls on northeast Baranof Island where the first run of chum salmon returned in fall 1981.

Above — The Alaska Lumber and Pulp Company mill opened at Silver Bay, five miles east of Sitka, in 1959. The mill has processed timber continuously since that time to produce dissolving pulp which is used for rayon products, cellophane, and camera film. (Rollo Pool, staff)

Left — At the log dump at Redoubt Bay, logs strapped in bundles are rolled into the water, to be towed to the mills. (Leo Evans)

The original residents of Baranof and Chichagof islands developed a culture based upon products from the sea and from the forest. Their mastery of the sea was made possible by materials from the forests. Natives hewed large canoes up to 60 feet in length, the best and largest made from western red cedar which was not native to either island. Smaller canoes were made from Sitka spruce. Houses were of spruce, hand-split planks covering log frames. Trees furnished most of the household, personal and ceremonial articles.

An increased demand for timber came with Russian colonization. Logs were cut for building forts. Wood provided houses, furniture, implements, barrels for flour and fish, firewood and ships. As the colony prospered, new construction required a continuing supply of logs and lumber as well as a constant supply of firewood and charcoal.

In the absence of coal, charcoal was used to melt the metals at the foundry. Stands of hemlock and spruce along Indian River were clear-cut, and charcoal was produced on the spot.

Shipbuilding was an important occupation in the colony. Alaska cedar was favored for hull construction; selective logging of yellow cedar took place along tidewater as far distant as Peril Strait.

At first lumber for the growing colony was hewn or sawn by hand, but water-powered sawmills soon appeared. The first Alaska sawmill is thought to have been built at Redoubt Bay in 1833 and was said to be the second built on the Pacific coast, the first having been erected by the Hudson's Bay Company on the Columbia River. The sawmill at Redoubt Bay first operated by water power and then was converted to steam power in the 1850s. Lumber was sawn for export as well as local use, and it is probable that a cargo of lumber carried to Chile in 1839 was sawn at the Redoubt mill.

Sawmills were operating in Sitka at the time of United States purchase. One mill, known as the American Russian Commercial Company, operated spasmodically for the next 60 years. Businessmen attempted to start another sawmill in the old Russian sail loft building; however, the machinery for the mill was removed in 1870.

Markets for timber products did not develop and for a few years in the early 1880s Sitka seems to have been without an active sawmill.

The old Russian mill reopened in 1888 and cut lumber for such things as planed sidewalks in Sitka. Then in 1889 John G. Brady and T.C. Doran built a new steam mill which operated off and on until 1905. Brady was a clergyman, businessman and lawyer who was U.S. Commissioner at Sitka from 1885 to 1888, and later became a territorial governor. Competition for the Brady-Doran operation began in 1893 when W.P. Mills repaired the old Russian mill which had been closed for a few years. These mills handled spruce

primarily, but a small amount of yellow cedar was processed for shipbuilding.

By the close of the 1800s, use of local lumber had increased as the fishing and mining industries gathered momentum. Growth within Alaska also helped. In the new town of Skagway in 1898, buildings of Sitka lumber began to take shape. At Valdez thousands of feet of Sitka lumber were received.

Logging in these early years was unique to Southeast Alaska. Practically all operations were from the beach. Handline and A-frames moved the huge trees from stands easily reached from protected shores. Loggers built strong floats for steam donkeys to provide

A passenger on the S.S. *Ancon* took this photo of an old Russian sawmill at Sitka in 1885. At that time the mill was run by water taken from Swan Lake and carried by the flume on the left and dropped onto the water wheel. (Alaska Historical Library)

years the mill cut lumber for canned and frozen fish boxes, fish trap cappings, cannery dock repairs and mining timbers, as well as for buildings.

The timber industry was tied for years to the fishing industry. Large quantities of hemlock were used for pilings and spruce for trap logs. This interrelationship did not end with the sale of products to each other. Many Alaskans who worked in seasonal fishing jobs found employment in the timber industry during a large part of the remainder of the year.

Another sawmill was built in Sitka in the mid-1930s. During the Depression Sheldon Jackson School felt the pinch, yet repairs to the Presbyterian school were needed. Enthusiastic instructors and their students constructed a sawmill from beachcombed odds and ends. Huge fir trees which had been squared off in the Lower 48 for shipment to Japan had been lost overboard during storms in the Gulf of Alaska. These washed ashore on Kruzof Island beaches and were towed to the beach in front of the school. Lumber was salvaged from construction of the Pioneers' Home. The students split cedar shakes for the roof. The old sawmill machinery from a mine up the Indian River valley was hauled to the school and reconditioned in machine shop classes. A diesel generator was donated from an abandoned cannery on Admiralty Island. The old log haul from the Brady mill was salvaged from the beach.

The Sheldon Jackson sawmill filled the demands for lumber at the school until the mill was destroyed by fire in 1940. Immediately plans were laid for reconstruction. The only thing salvageable was the Brady log haul, which served the rebuilt mill throughout the 1940s and 1950s. When in the 1960s the mill fell to disuse, all the equipment except the

power, bunkhouses, cookhouses and blacksmith shops. Gas boats towed the outfit and then brought the log rafts to town. In the early 1900s logs came from such places as the head of Krestof Island, northwest of Sitka, and Fish Bay on the northwest coast of Baranof Island, north of Sitka.

At Fish Bay in 1917 it was announced that the first permanent logging camp in Alaska would be built. Logs were hauled on a pole road which tapped the valley for three miles from the head of the bay.

The W.P. Mills sawmill (the old Russian mill) was sold in early 1924 and reopened again in March of that year. In the following

Aerial grass seeding is part of Alaska Lumber and Pulp Company's logging program. Grass seed is applied near roadsides at logging operations for erosion prevention and aesthetic purposes. (Leo Evans)

93

A small sawmill operated between 1913 and 1918 at the base of a waterfall in Warm Springs Bay, on the east coast of Baranof Island. The mill reportedly harvested mostly yellow cedar.
(Patricia Roppel collection)

Brady log haul was sold. The space is now used for the college's aquaculture program.

Sitka's other sawmill, that of W.P. Mills, was sold to Columbia Lumber Company which supplied lumber during the war years for construction of military facilities on Japonski Island and other nearby islands.

Other sawmills operated intermittently on Baranof and Chichagof islands, harvesting timber and sawing it into dimension lumber. To provide necessary materials for the mining camps at Rodman Bay and Chichagof, each company put in a sawmill which lasted the life of the mining operation.

An attempt was made to start a mill at Pavlof Harbor, but it is doubtful this effort got past the stage where water power was developed. At Suloia Bay, at the west end of Peril Strait on the southwest coast of Chichagof Island, a factory for cutting and making salmon boxes was built in 1918, but was dismantled the following year. Hidden Falls Lumber Company on Kasnyku Bay had more success. Here a partnership of four men — Ben Ficken, Linus Carlson, John Maurstad and Harold Shaffer — operated a mill from 1929 to 1931 when the Depression caught up with the operation. A sawmill ran from 1913 to 1918 at the base of the spectacular waterfall in Warm Springs Bay on Baranof's east coast. This mill reportedly harvested mostly yellow cedar, which was selectively cut in nearby forests and skidded out on the snow.

The U.S. Forest Service sought to attract the paper industry to Alaska soon after World War I. Although it took many years, these efforts to establish pulp mills breathed new life into the timber industry on Baranof and Chichagof islands. Japanese interests formed the Alaska Lumber and Pulp Company as the first major foreign investment made by Japan after World War II. The company was awarded a 50-year cutting right to 4.49 billion board feet of timber located on Baranof Island and portions of Chichagof Island in 1956. Their pulp mill opened in Silver Bay in 1959 and has processed timber continuously since that time to produce dissolving pulp, the high grade pulp used for rayon products, cellophane and camera film.

Logging areas are scattered throughout the region. The average logging camps — 50 to 60 men plus their families — resemble small towns with grade schools, movies and recreation facilities. Communication is via radio and transportation via air taxi services. Camps are

located at Corner Bay in Tenakee Inlet, Kennel Creek in Freshwater Bay and at Salt Lake in Port Frederick.

Today Sitka has a small sawmill in Jamestown Bay where residents can purchase rough lumber, but many building supplies are shipped in from the Lower 48. The Brady log haul sits near the Sheldon Jackson College campus. Plans continue to return it to the original site of the Brady sawmill where the log haul will be restored as a reminder of the early days of Sitka's timber industry.

A familiar sight in Sitka is a log raft being towed through the harbor on its way to the Silver Bay site of Alaska Lumber and Pulp Company's mill. (Darrel Barfield)

Right — Logging areas are scattered throughout the region. At some, the loggers and their families make their homes in floating logging camps, such as this one at Redoubt Bay. (Leo Evans)

Gold. The lure that drew the adventurous across the prairies and into the most remote gullies in the western states played an important role in the Sitka area as well. Some of these adventurous men who came north soon after Alaska's purchase made the first attempts at lode mining in the vicinity of Sitka beginning in 1871.

A year later, in 1872, three Sitka men trudged through the forest near the head of Silver Bay and came upon a gold-bearing quartz ledge. Inexperience caused them to consider the outcrop worthless. Nicholas Haley, a member of the Sitka garrison who had worked in mines in California, saw some of the gold and was spurred to locate what became known as the Stewart Ledge, named for Maj. Joseph Stewart of the U.S. Army. This discovery prompted a rush by others in Sitka and before 1880 — when gold was discovered at present-day Juneau — many ledges were staked in the hills around Silver Bay.

All of the gold was in hard rock. Placer mining has always attracted the greatest number of miners because the returns are nearly immediate and can be obtained by anyone with a grubstake, rocker, pan, pick, shovel and boundless energy. No great stampede occurred in Sitka to the hard rock gold.

However, men banded together to form companies and raise capital to extract the gold from the earth. George Pilz erected a 10-stamp mill on the Stewart claim in 1879. This was Alaska's first stamp mill to process gold ore. Investors spent considerable money to develop the Silver Bay properties during the next two decades, but a comedy of disastrous mismanagement prevented success. Some ore was known to have been milled, but there is no record of the amount of gold recovered.

During the years after the Silver Bay discoveries, some gold claims were located in the

area. From attempts to develop these claims came some remarkable mining failures. Those at Pande Basin, near Sitka, and Rodman Bay, on Baranof's northeast coast, became well known. Tremendous outlays of money were made on transportation systems such as the seven-mile-long railroad at Rodman Bay. Expensive equipment was shipped for far more grandiose operations than the deposits warranted. Only after vast capital had been spent did investors realize the actual value of the mines, and by then it was too late to get a return on investments.

These failures led to the nearly complete extinction of interest in lode mining in the Sitka district. Mining in the area lapsed into dormancy.

Gypsum and not gold instigated the revival of mining interest and the era of commercial mining in the Sitka district. Work began in 1902 at Iyoukeen Cove, on the northeastern corner of Chichagof Island. Production started in 1906, continuing with brief interruptions for 17 years as Alaska's only commercial producer of gypsum.

Interest in gold revived in 1905 when the glittery mineral was discovered in a stream at the head of Klag Bay on Chichagof's west coast. A Native fisherman who went ashore for water noticed gold in one of the numerous quartz fragments. The fisherman sought aid from Sitka merchants, and the group quickly located the outcropping. A small stampede ensued.

Thus began the years when the Sitka area was an important contributor to gold production in Southeast Alaska. Mines on southwestern Chichagof Island were second only to mines near Juneau in total lode-gold production in Alaska. From the time the lodes were discovered in 1905 until mining was ordered suspended during World War II, more than

three-quarters of a million ounces of gold and a
small amount of silver were recovered, mostly
from the Chichagof Mine near Klag Bay and
the Hirst-Chichagof Mine in Kimshan Cove.
Two or three dozen other prospects in the area
were explored to some extent, but none
reached production.

The mines were located on landlocked harbors protected from the open ocean. To reach
these quiet waters, ships, laden with the
necessities to build and then to maintain and
supply the large mining camps of Chichagof
and Hirst-Chichagof, traversed 10 to 20 miles
of reef-infested, open waters. On the return
trip freighters hauled the gold-and-silver
concentrates.

At the large mines, bunkhouses, houses for
families, showers and dry rooms, a store,
docks and assay offices surrounded the gigan-
tic mill buildings. Chichagof Mine also had a
well-equipped hospital and a large club house.

The mining camp at the Hirst-Chichagof Mine in Kimshan Cove was constructed in 1920, and the mill began operating in 1922. About 100 people lived at the mine, which was closed during World War II. Attempts to reopen Hirst-Chichagof were unsuccessful, and the buildings burned in the mid-1950s.
(U.S. Geological Survey)

As many as 200 people lived at Chichagof; about half that many at Hirst-Chichagof.

Activities at Chichagof started nearly 15 years before the Hirst-Chichagof mill and camp began in earnest. At Chichagof, tunnels were driven, and ore was crushed and concentrated in a 30-stamp mill. The pure free gold was poured into bricks. One $23,000 brick was stolen by two masked bandits from the room above the company store. The robbers were caught but, because the snow was deep, the hiding place of the brick was not discovered for nearly a month.

After World War II, when the War Production Board stopped all gold mining, various attempts were made to rejuvenate the mining. But these efforts never restored the earlier degree of mining in the area.

Of the other mining operations at the Sitka area, perhaps the most productive were those of the Apex and El Nido deposits across Lisian-ski Inlet from Pelican. The adjoining properties were worked together, and the mine operators crushed the gold-bearing quartz to extract the precious mineral for 15 years from 1924 to 1939. The Apex-El Nido, as the operation was called, also produced respectable quantities of tungsten as well as gold.

Less glamorous minerals also occur in the Sitka district, however, none except gypsum have been mined commercially. At Snipe Bay a low-grade deposit of nickel-copper spurred interest. Chromite occurs on Baranof Island with the largest lode at Red Bluff Bay on the eastern shore. Copper-nickel deposits were explored extensively near Mirror Harbor on Chichagof Island and in Bohemia Basin on the east side of Yakobi Island. The latter deposit, known as the Takanis ore body, is estimated to be worth millions of dollars if developed.

Mining has not provided many jobs in the Baranof and Chichagof islands during recent

Left — The Pinta Bay Mining Company attempted to develop a gold and copper prospect at the head of Goulding Harbor on Chichagof Island in the 1920s. A five-mile railroad with a "Fordson" locomotive — built from a Ford tractor — was used to haul supplies to the camp on the mountainside. A small amount of ore was produced at the mine. (A.F. Buddington, 153, U.S. Geological Survey)

Left — Joe Bower's cabin still stands at Radioville, on a small island at the entrance to Khaz Bay. Bower contracted with both Chichagof and Hirst-Chichagof mines to handle wireless communications, as both mines were so shut in by mountains that signals were poor. An outboard skiff was used to deliver messages to and from the mines. (Ernest Robertson)

years. Exploration, however, is on the upsurge. Gold, with its increased value since the heydays at Chichagof and Hirst-Chichagof, is still being actively sought at such places as Cobol in Slocum Arm on the southwest coast of Chichagof and at Silver Bay. At the Bohemia Basin copper-nickel deposit development work continues.

Many people come to Baranof and Chichagof islands for outdoor recreation: hunting, fishing, boating, camping, picnicking and beachcombing. Sheltered marine waterways and numerous inland lakes allow boat and aircraft access to most areas of recreational interest. However, access is often difficult over much of the land because of steep terrain and dense vegetation. Consequently, much recreational use occurs within a mile of the beach, along rivers and streams, around fly-in lakes and on lands accessible by road or trail.

For 27 years Sitka has sponsored an annual salmon derby. In past years the winning fish has weighed as much as 73 pounds, 6 ounces, or as little as 50 pounds, 8 ounces. Salt-water fishing for bottom fish and halibut, capturing crabs in net traps and digging for clams at low tide are also popular.

For fishermen and others who want to spend several days in the wilderness, the U.S. Forest Service rents recreational cabins on a reservation basis. Some of the cabins are on high mountain lakes and must be reached by plane.

Other cabins are reached on foot from nearby harbors. One such cabin is at White Sulphur Springs on west Chichagof Island.

Waters from Betty and Jetty lakes tumble over this falls as they rush toward Port Armstrong. Electricity generated by this rushing water supplies power for a nearby hatchery. (Tom Paul)

Right — Log strewn beaches, forested mountains and numerous islands are typical of the Sitka Sound area. (Ueli Ackermann)

Here a heavy surf pounds the rocky coast and care must be taken to visit the springs in calm weather. Many fly in to a small lake nearby and hike to the cabin. A hot mineral springs is located above a small cove in which much driftwood is cast up on a beach of large, rounded stones. Various log bathhouses have been built over the principal springs, and in earlier years occasional hunters and trappers camped here. At that time the pools were called Hoonah Warm Springs, but years ago they were renamed for a dentist, Dr. White. In 1916 the U.S. Forest Service built its first cabin and bathhouse here. This cabin has been modernized in recent years so bathers can pull back a translucent "shoji-like" fiberglass screen and admire a view of the often turbulent Pacific Ocean while soaking in the hot water.

Other bathhouses are at Goddard, 16 miles south of Sitka on the outer coast of Baranof Island. Known as Sitka Hot Springs, this may have been the earliest Alaska mineral springs known to the Europeans. Sir George Simpson, governor-in-chief of Hudson's Bay Company's North American territories, visited the springs in 1841. He told of three cottages used as a hospital for invalids from Sitka. Natives, he said, came from "two or three hundred miles to benefit from the healing waters."

About 20 years after Alaska's purchase, an enterprising Sitka firm erected frame buildings for the use of people seeking the mineral water's benefits. By the 1920s a three-story hotel was built to provide more sophisticated accommodations. This building was purchased by the 1939 Territorial Legislature as an overflow home for the Sitka Pioneers' Home. Until 1946 many old-time Alaskans lived at Goddard during the seven years it was an auxiliary Pioneers' Home. After that the building fell into disuse and was finally torn

Clockwise from right —
■ Numerous lakes provide tranquil surroundings for boaters. Here, a canoe has been packed in to Sashin Lake, about eight miles north of Port Alexander. (Roger Vallion)

■ Campers enjoy the U.S. Forest Service cabin at Baranof Lake. Several such cabins are available on both Baranof and Chichagof islands, and may be rented for a nominal fee for up to a week. (Stephen E. Hilson)

■ Backpackers rest beside Crescent Harbor in Sitka. The forest service maintains several trails for hiking in the Sitka vicinity. (Staff)

■ Goddard Hot Springs, 16 miles south of Sitka, may have been the earliest Alaska mineral springs known to the Europeans. Today, the property is owned by the city of Sitka, which maintains two modern bathhouses there for recreational use. (Ernest Manewal)

■ Sitka Hot Springs at Goddard was developed by early 1920 to include this three-story hotel with 35 rooms, all heated with mineral water. The reputed curative powers of the springs was reported as far back as the Russian period. (Tongass Historical Society Museum)

Clockwise from top — A lucky angler has hooked this sockeye with a sport lure near Port Herbert. (Tom Paul)

■ A hunter prepares lunch at his camp, high on Baranof Island. A few hardy souls venture into the rugged high country in search of mountain goats. (R.E. Johnson)

■ Fishing gear in hand, Richard Mathews heads for a day of sport fishing on the east coast of Baranof Island. Once a fisherman, Mathews is now head of the hatchery project at Port Armstrong. (Tom Paul)

106

down. Today the city of Sitka owns the property and maintains two modern bathhouses for recreational use. On nearby private land, a few people live year-round.

Hunters search the rugged peaks of Baranof Island for the transplanted mountain goats. Here too opportunities abound for hikes, but the difficulties of reaching the alpine tundra make these areas where few venture.

A series of more accessible trails are maintained by the U.S. Forest Service. From Sitka,

hikers can make day trips up the Indian River toward its source in a cirque under sharply pointed peaks between The Sisters and Arrowhead Peak; to the top of Mount Verstovia, which dominates Sitka's eastern horizon; to Thimbleberry and Beaver lakes, both examples of moderate elevation lakes surrounded by rain forest; to Gavan Hill, a dominant feature on the northern Sitka skyline.

Other trails require a boat or floatplane to reach the trail head at salt water. Most of these trails lead to forest service cabins. One at Baranof Warm Springs wends its way past the

falls to Baranof Lake. Another starts at Silver Bay and ends four and a half miles later at the upper reaches of Redoubt Lake. Kruzof Island can be crossed from Mud Bay to the outer coast beach at Shelikof Bay, along a six-mile trail. Starting from the old Chatham cannery ruins, a four-mile trail follows Sitkoh Creek to the lake providing opportunities for fishing coho, pink, sockeye salmon, cutthroat trout and Dolly Varden. In Suloia Bay a short trail leads to a cabin on Lake Suloia within the West Chichagof-Yakobi Wilderness.

A seven-mile trail, designated as a National Recreational Trail, begins at Fred's Creek on Kruzof Island and leads up Mount Edgecumbe to its crater. The trail crosses several patches of muskeg, then steepens for the final climb to the volcano. Future plans, when funds become available, are to expand this trail system to the abandoned army camp, caves and fumaroles near Shoals Point. This would give hikers the option of short treks or extensive expeditions of several weeks.

Bluewater paddling — travel by hand-powered craft such as canoes or kayaks through the tidal waters along the coast — can provide challenging experiences. These waters, however, are characterized by extreme tidal fluctuations, cold temperatures, strong currents and frequent high winds and waves. The careful traveler will find solitude and splendor among the numerous small islands. Occasional portages such as the one between Tenakee Inlet and Port Frederick open up sheltered bluewater trips. This trip can be started from either Hoonah or Tenakee Springs, both served by the Alaska Marine Highway System.

Throughout the area these and other recreational opportunities abound for those who take the time to plan for careful and wise use of what nature has provided.

The Alaska state ferry *LeConte* waits at the dock at Hoonah. The ferries provide access to starting points for sheltered bluewater paddling trips. (Lael Morgan, staff, reprinted from *ALASKA GEOGRAPHIC®*)

Still rich in both Tlingit and Russian culture, the Sitka of today is a thriving, modern city of 7,803. State revenue sharing records report the Sitka borough (Baranof Island and the southern half of Chichagof Island) population as 8,787.

Alaska Airlines provides interregional scheduled flights to Sitka, and Alaska Marine Highway ferries serve Sitka eight times weekly during the tourist season and four times weekly during the winter. Bush planes and smaller boats bring residents from outlying areas into town to connect with transportation out of the region.

In addition to the timber industry and fishing, tourism generates a substantial portion of Sitka's revenue. One hundred cruise ships from at least five different lines call at this former Russian capital. Visitors find many relics of the Tlingit and Russian periods to explore. Dominating Sitka's main street is Saint Michael's Cathedral. Originally the cathedral was built of thick logs of Sitka spruce covered with dark gray clapboard, a style of architecture found in Russia near Saint Petersburg. The cathedral stood for 118 years before a tragic fire in 1966 destroyed it. Immediately plans were laid to rebuild Saint Michael's in its original size and style, using the original blueprints preserved since 1848. The cathedral collection, saved from the fire by zealous citizens, includes eucharistic vessels, vestments, chalice covers and many icons which date back to the time of Russian America.

Above — O'Connell Bridge, 1,225 feet long, connects Sitka with Japonski Island. Dedicated in 1972, it is the first cable-stayed, girder span bridge built in the United States. (Pat Roppel)

Right — Bush planes are a common means of travel from Sitka to outlying communities. Snow is being swept off the wings of this De Havilland Beaver. (R.E. Johnson)

Opposite — This view of Sitka's waterfront was taken from the U.S. Coast Guard dock on Japonski Island. The large green and white structure at right is the Alaska Native Brotherhood Hall, built in 1914. The hall is listed on the National Register of Historic Places. (Stephen E. Hilson)

After the burning of the cathedral, one of the few original buildings to survive from Russian days is the Russian Bishop's House. More popularly known as The Orphanage, the building was built in 1842 as a residence, office and private chapel to Veniaminov, a man famous in the annals of the Russian church who was later Metropolitan of Moscow and chief among Russian bishops. The first floor served as an office, archives, school and domicile for the bishop's staff. On the second floor were the bishop's living quarters and his chapel, The Church of the Annunciation. A seminary to train Natives as Russian Orthodox priests was conducted here for a number of years. After the transfer of Russian America to the United States, funds for the Russian church no longer were sent, and by the mid-1880s the building needed repairs.

In 1962 the Russian Bishop's House became a Registered National Historical Landmark, and 10 years later the house became part of Sitka National Historical Park. The National Park Service has undertaken an extensive restoration program. When restoration is completed, visitors will have an opportunity to see a structure built about 140 years ago by the Russians and to view the bishop's residence, chapel and library.

Other reminders of Russian days can be found throughout Sitka: the Blarney Stone, where Baranov is said to have rested on his walks; the replica of the Russian blockhouse, like those in the stockade which once separated the Russian and Tlingit sections of Sitka; Russian cannons once used to guard the Russian America capital; the grave of Princess Maksoutoff, wife of the last governor of the Russian colony; Castle Hill, site of the October 1867 transfer of sovereignty to the United States and once location of the governor's residence; and the Russian cemetery.

The collection of totem poles at the Sitka National Historical Park (above and left) was gathered from Tlingit and Haida villages on Prince of Wales Island in 1904 for the Louisiana Purchase Exposition in St. Louis. The poles were returned to Sitka following the show, and now stand along paths among the giant spruce and hemlock trees as part of the park. (Above, Sharon Paul, staff; left, Stephen E. Hilson)

Lower left — The Russian Bishop's House, also known as The Orphanage, is undergoing extensive repairs to restore it as closely as possible to its appearance in 1843-1867. The structure is a Registered National Historic Place, and is part of the Sitka National Historical Park. (Rollo Pool, staff)

Right — The New Archangel Dancers perform traditional folk dances for visitors. (Tim Thompson, reprinted from ALASKA® magazine)

The Prospector, a 13½-foot clay and bronze statue, has been a fixture in front of the Sitka Pioneers' Home since 1949. Sculptor Victor Alonzo Lewis modeled the statue after a true pioneer, William "Skagway Bill" Fonda. This 1980 photo shows two workers as they give The Prospector his first cleaning in 31 years. (Rollo Pool, staff, reprinted from *ALASKA*® magazine)

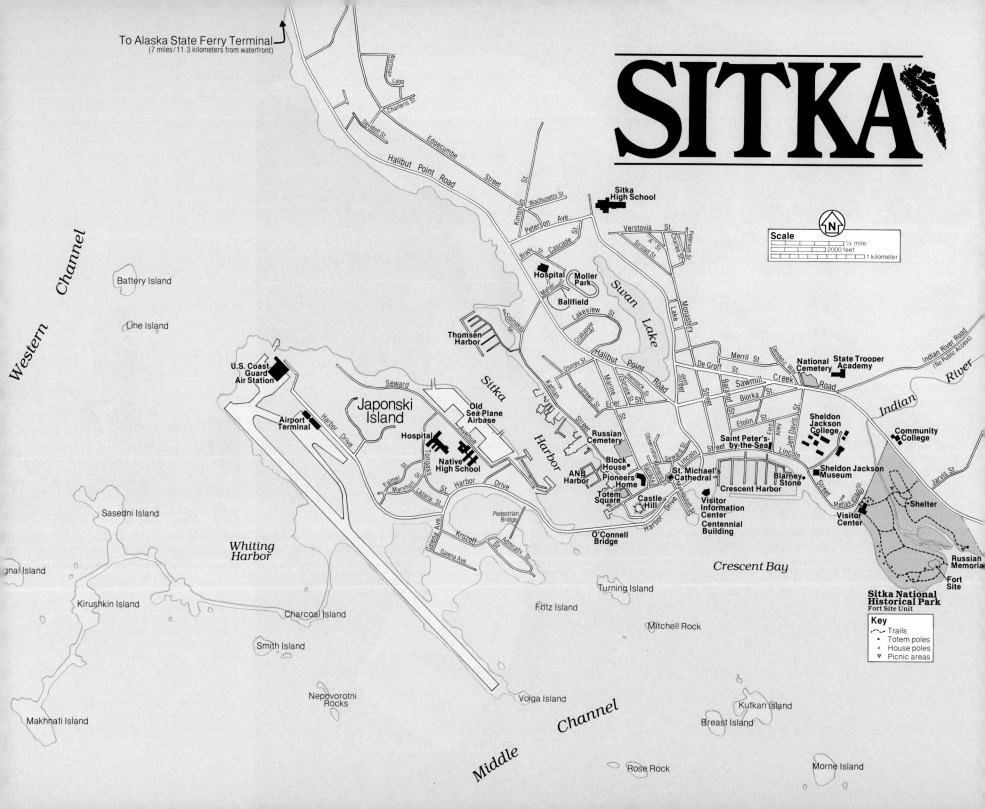

SITKA

To Alaska State Ferry Terminal
(7 miles/11.3 kilometers from waterfront)

Wortman Loop

Charters St.

Davidoff St.

Edgecumbe Street

Halibut Point Road

Kimshan St.

Wachusetts St.

Sitka High School

Peterson Ave.

Brady St.

Cascade St.

Verstovia St.

"A" St.

Sirstad St.

Charles St.

Peterson St.

Monastery

Scale
½ mile
2000 feet
1 kilometer

N

Hospital

Moller Park

Moller St.

Ballfield

Lakeview St.

Crabapple St.

Swan Lake

Lake

Western Channel

Battery Island

Line Island

Seloinakau St.

Thomsen Harbor

Halibut

Point

Osprey St.

Merril St.

De Groff St.

Genedic Way

Sawmill Creek

Indian River Road
(No Public Access)

National Cemetery

State Trooper Academy

Road

Indian

River

U.S. Coast Guard Air Station

Seward

Sitka

Barandi St.

Biorka St.

Sheldon Jackson College

Community College

Japonski Island

Airport Terminal

Harbor Drive

Old Sea Plane Airbase

Tongass Avenue

Hospital

Native High School

Harbor

Kallan St.

Andrews St.

Marine St.

Erler St.

Hemlock St.

Spruce St.

Etolin St.

Russian Cemetery

Saint Peter's-by-the-Sea

Jeff Davis St.

Sheldon Jackson Museum

Palmer St.

Marshall St.

Lazaria St.

Harbor

Drive

Observatory St.

American St.

Seward St.

Lincoln St.

Block House

Pioneers Home

ANB Harbor

Finn Alley

St. Michael's Cathedral

Crescent Harbor

Blarney Stone

Metlakatla St.

Galena Ave.

Kruzoff St.

Admiralty St.

Pedestrian Bridge

Totem Square

Barracks St.

Katlian St.

Castle Hill

Harbor Drive

Lincoln St.

Visitor Information Center

Centennial Building

Visitor Center

Shelter

Jarvis St.

Galena Ave.

O'Connell Bridge

Whiting Harbor

Sasedni Island

Signal Island

Kirushkin Island

Makhnati Island

Turning Island

Crescent Bay

Fritz Island

Mitchell Rock

Russian Memorial

Fort Site

Sitka National Historical Park
Fort Site Unit

Key
- - - Trails
• Totem poles
+ House poles
▽ Picnic areas

Smith Island

Nepovorotni Rocks

Charcoal Island

Volga Island

Middle Channel

Rose Rock

Breast Island

Kutkan Island

Morne Island

This aerial photo was taken during a routine, high altitude, NASA mapping flight.

Old Sitka

Ferry Terminal

Middle Island

Halibut Point

Halibut Point Road

Halibut Mountain

Map Location

Baranof Island

Indian River

N

Price St.

Lance St.

Sawmill Creek Road

Japonski Island

Sitka

Sawmill Creek Road

Pulp Mill

Pulp Mill

Cannon Island

Sitka Sound

Sawmill Creek Road

Eastern Channel

The Tlingit heritage is still evident and has survived despite the adverse effects of a long period during which their society was dominated by a colonial power.

Today Native totemic art and culture are preserved and interpreted at Sitka National Historical Park. Here Tlingit Indians fortified themselves in their palisaded fort against the Russians from the battleship *Neva*. After the Russians landed, the fort was burned; archaeologists found the charred logs when excavating the old wall in 1958. Today the fort is outlined by white stakes. The battle site was reserved as a public park in 1890, but not until 1910 was it set aside as a national monument by presidential proclamation.

The Sitka Tlingits did not erect totem poles in front of their homes. The collection at Sitka National Historical Park was gathered from Haida and Tlingit villages on Prince of Wales Island during the governorship of John Brady for the 1904 Louisiana Purchase Exposition in St. Louis. At the exposition, models of two Haida houses were constructed with Native poles on the front and side. After the show, Governor Brady had the poles brought to Sitka. They silently stand today among the giant spruce and hemlock trees along a needle-strewn path.

Complementing the valuable exhibits of Tlingit and Russian artifacts at Sitka National Historical Park is the Indian Cultural Center. Here Tlingits demonstrate beadwork, silverwork and wood carving as they answer visitors' questions. In addition they pass on techniques, knowledge and traditions by teaching others.

A fine collection of Indian and Eskimo artifacts is housed at the Sheldon Jackson College campus. A missionary, Dr. Sheldon Jackson traveled throughout Alaska during the 1880s as an educator. He saw the value of preserving

Clockwise from right —
■ Every year on Alaska Day, October 18, a Russian flag is raised and replaced by the American flag during a ceremony for which Sitka residents dress up in period costumes. The ceremony is part of three days of festivities celebrating the anniversary of the United States' purchase of Alaska from Russia. (Lael Morgan, staff)

■ A fire on January 2, 1966, destroyed Saint Michael's Cathedral, the Lutheran Church and many business buildings in downtown Sitka. Saint Michael's was rebuilt, using the original blueprints, as a fireproof replica of the Russian-built structure. (Martin Strand)

■ The Sheldon Jackson Museum was established in 1888 to house native art, artifacts and other items of historical interest collected by Dr. Sheldon Jackson during his travels. The present building, the first concrete building in Alaska, was built in 1895 to provide a fireproof home for the treasures. (Patricia Roppel)

■ The Centennial Building, dedicated on the 100th anniversary of Alaska's purchase, is the hub for all visitors and conventions in Sitka. A Tlingit ceremonial canoe stands in front of the building, decorated with an eagle-raven design by Sitka artist George Benson. Inside the building, the Sitka Historical Society's museum exhibits memorabilia of the city's lively days. (Far right, Matt Donohoe; right, Rollo Pool, staff)

Above — A logger participates in the speed climbing competition at the All-Alaska Logging Championship in Sitka.
(R.E. Johnson)

Opposite — The springs at Baranof, on Warm Springs Bay, were developed around 1910 as a health resort. Today, Baranof consists of a small family operated store and a bathhouse.
(Stephen E. Hilson)

Native artifacts and in 1888 built the first museum in the territory to house his collection and other items of historical significance.

Another collection and display of Sitka's vivid past is that of the Sitka Historical Society. Artifacts of every aspect of Sitka's past give an idea of what Sitka and its residents were like. Housed in the Centennial Building, the museum is run by volunteers of the society.

The Centennial Building, dedicated on the 100th anniversary of Alaska's purchase, is the hub for all visitors and conventions. Perhaps best known of these gatherings is the Sitka Summer Music Festival held each June since 1971. Some of the world's finest musicians return year after year to perform. The large glass windows behind the stage provide a breathtaking view of Sitka Sound and the forest and mountains. Music lovers travel from all over the United States to join Sitka residents in nights filled with the world's masterpieces of chamber music.

Alaska Day, October 18, is marked with three days of festivities. Sitka residents dress in period costumes and act out speeches and presentations made during the transfer of Alaska from Russia to the United States. Each year a Russian flag is raised and replaced by the American flag during the afternoon ceremony.

Each July Sitka hosts the All-Alaska Logging Championships which feature such contests as ax chopping and speed climbing. Most competition is aimed toward experienced loggers, but the rolling pin toss, nail driving and Ma and Pa bucking always add a note of humor.

For residents of Sitka the historical treasures and annual events are a background to everyday activities.

About 500 of Sitka's residents work at the pulp mill at Silver Bay; the rest are employed primarily in government, as fishermen or at Sitka's two fish processing plants, in tourism or the usual commercial activities. The town has no major department stores but does have two supermarkets and an assortment of smaller shops. Three hotels and one motel provide a total of about 300 rooms, and several restaurants serve visitors and residents. In addition to Sheldon Jackson College and a community college, Sitka has a high school, a junior high and three elementary schools.

The Alaska Department of Public Safety maintains a training academy in Sitka, and the U.S. Coast Guard operates an air station there. Sitka is also home port for the U.S. Coast Guard vessel *Woodrush* which tends navigational aids in Southeast as well as helps with search and rescue.

In late 1981 Green Lake Dam, south of Sitka, was completed to provide additional power for the city. An earlier dam was completed in 1959 for the pulp mill, and a third dam is scheduled for completion in 1989 at Takatz Lake on the east coast of Baranof Island.

Shee Atika, Inc., one of several urban corporations established under the Alaska Native Claims Settlement Act, represents the interests of Sitka's Tlingits. The corporation was formed in 1974 and concentrates its efforts in forest resources management, tourism and fisheries. Shee Atika owns a hotel in Sitka, and has 3,000 acres at Katlian Bay where it will plant trees for harvesting in future years. By summer 1982 Shee Atika expects to have title to two islands, Alice and Charcoal, near Sitka, which are appropriate for residential and commercial development. The corporation's nonprofit arm is looking toward aquaculture development such as salmon hatcheries and enhancement programs.

Above — The small community of Port Alexander spreads out along the shores of a bay with the same name just north of Cape Ommaney on the Chatham Strait side of Baranof Island's southern tip. A cold storage facility and restaurant, which operate in the summer, and a store and post office, open year-round but not necessarily five days a week, supply the needs for the town's 100 or so residents who enjoy a quiet, relaxed lifestyle. (Tom Paul)

Left — Many of the town's approximately 100 residents turn out for mail day twice a week at Port Alexander. (Tom Paul)

Outside of Sitka, few communities break the solitude of the Baranof and Chichagof wilderness.

After a land sale in 1971, new homes were built, cabins repaired and fish processing revived at Port Alexander, five miles north of Cape Ommaney at the southern tip of Baranof Island. Today residents work at fishing, at a nearby fish hatchery, man the post office or subsist and enjoy the quiet of their isolated community of about 100 people.

Along the eastern shore of Baranof and Chichagof islands between Port Alexander and the next large community of Tenakee Springs is Baranof in Warm Springs Bay. Here a family operated store and fueling station cater to recreational boaters and an occasional fisherman. The springs were developed around 1910 as a health resort. A visitor in 1915 reported three bathhouses, one of which had six wooden tubs. Records indicate the area receives considerable snowfall, but winter temperatures are not extreme and in the early days some people spent the winter at the springs.

Another hot springs, Tenakee Springs (population 154) in Tenakee Inlet on Chichagof Island, has attracted people since before the turn of the century. A quiet wintering spot for prospectors and miners, Tenakee began to cater to cannery workers and fishermen when two or three nearby canneries, some for salmon and some for crab, were packing seafood. The Purple Onion and the Shamrock Bar provided liquid refreshments. The Liberty Theater, a laundry and restaurants were part of the thriving community. Today Tenakee Springs is mostly a retirement community, although a few young families have built new homes here. People from Juneau and Sitka have built cabins there or renovated the earlier sturdy ones built by

Above — Forlorn buildings in 1948 tell of Port Alexander's decline when the salmon disappeared a few years earlier. (Courtesy of R.H. Gorr)

Right — A waterfall cascades down a hill near Warm Springs Bay. The falls provided power for a sawmill which operated there for several years in the early 1900s. (Stephen E. Hilson)

Left — Rick Paul attaches crossbeams to a cornerpost during construction of a cabin at Port Alexander. (Tom Paul)

Finnish residents years ago. Tenakee's population now booms in the summer.

The town's economy depends on subsistence and commercial fishing. A logging camp at Corner Bay, directly across the inlet, started in 1973 and now provides employment for some Tenakee residents. Corner Bay residents shop at Tenakee's store and enjoy baths in the hot springs. However, the lifestyle of most Tenakee Springs people continues to depend on isolation, simplicity and enjoyment of natural surroundings.

Rapidly growing Hoonah (population 677) lies near the mouth of Port Frederick on Chichagof's north coast. Long before the Europeans came, a group of Tlingits, the Hoonahs, fished the rocky shores near the permanent village of Hoonah "the place where the north-wind does not blow." Shallow lines were used for salmon and deeper ones for halibut. For a brief time fur hunting and trapping were prof-

Clockwise from left —

■ Tenakee Springs, built around a hot springs on Tenakee Inlet, has attracted people since before the turn of the century. Once a thriving community, today Tenakee is primarily a retirement town, with a population of 154. (Rollo Pool, staff)

■ Flowers brighten up the front of a Tenakee Springs resident's home in the center of town. Most of Tenakee's buildings line the waterfront. (Rollo Pool, staff)

■ Late afternoon light illuminates the houses along the main street of Hoonah, a Tlingit community on the north end of Chichagof Island. Tour boats depart from here for Glacier Bay, which some legends claim is the ancestral home of many Tlingit people, including those at Hoonah. (Rollo Pool, staff)

121

Above and right — Hoonah's economy has traditionally been supported by fisheries. The waterfront is lined with fish processors, boats tied to floats and a few old vessels abandoned on the beach.
(Rollo Pool, staff)

itable. When the fur trade declined, Hoonah residents returned to fishing. Salmon and crab canneries and mild cure stations operated in Hoonah at various times, and today many of the town's residents continue this tradition. Modern cold storages process the fishing fleet's harvest. Although the seine fleet has experienced severe economic difficulties through intermittent closure of adjacent waters, the seiners operate in other areas for limited periods. Subsistence fishing exists for only a small troll fleet, many of which are hand trollers.

The village corporation, Huna Totem Corporation, has interim land conveyance from the Alaska Native Claims Settlement Act, and the community regards future development of timber holdings as a major economic opportunity.

A proposed road system between the logging operations in the Whitestone Harbor

and Freshwater Bay areas is expected to create local employment in the future and will increase access to recreational areas.

This proposed logging and road building on northeastern Chichagof Island represent major impacts and opportunities for Hoonah. Community leaders recognize the effects on their social, economic and culture structure which may result as population increases and new employment patterns emerge.

At the mouth of Game Creek, a few miles south of Hoonah, is Mount Bether Bible Center. Founded in recent years as a Christian community, Game Creek, as it is known locally, is an agricultural community. Through extensive enrichment of the land using kelp, shell and refuse from the Hoonah fish processing plants, crops have been sufficiently abundant to permit marketing, primarily in Hoonah and Juneau, of produce beyond the community's needs. Using a small

Left — The settlement of Game Creek, also known as Mount Bether Bible Center, is located a few miles south of Hoonah. The residents of this agricultural community keep a herd of cattle, possibly the only herd on Baranof or Chichagof island. (R.E. Johnson)

Middle — Winter does not slow the activities of Game Creek's energetic residents. Founded in 1975, the people there have accomplished extensive enrichment of the land using kelp, shells and refuse from Hoonah's fish processing plants. Crops produced in excess of the community's needs are marketed in Hoonah and Juneau. (R.E. Johnson)

Above — Game Creek residents operate a small community sawmill, which provides lumber for community buildings. (Marty Loken)

123

From left to right —

■ The troller *Haley Christine* sits on the grid at Pelican. The town, which has a present population of 180, was started in the 1940s by fish buyer Kalle Raatikainen, who wanted a processing plant closer to the surrounding fishing grounds. (Matt Donohoe)

■ Fishermen often gather on the dock to meet friends, tell stories and offer advice. Here, Capt. Billy Stalneker of the troller *Defiance* gives a haircut to his friend, Capt. John Garth of the *Lady Ruth*, on the dock at Pelican. (Chip Porter)

■ Rosie's Bar and Grill, an institution for many years in Pelican, is a popular gathering place for residents and area fishermen. (Chip Porter)

■ Pelican resident "Papa Joe" Paddock stands on the boardwalk that runs along the main part of town. Most of Pelican is built over the water on pilings. (Matt Donohoe)

community sawmill, Game Creek residents have constructed their own homes, work buildings and a large meeting hall-school. Residents plan to construct a road spur to a proposed logging road which would give them access to Hoonah and its link with the marine ferry system.

Another community faced with the possibility of change is Pelican, on Lisianski Inlet on Chichagof Island. This small fishing village of 180 residents is near the proposed nickel-copper mine at Bohemia Basin on Yakobi Island. Plans for the mine's development are still uncertain. However, if the mine should be put on a production basis, Pelican is the nearest service area. Pelican is also a jumping off point for the West Chichagof-Yakobi Wilderness.

Built mainly over the water on pilings, with a boardwalk, Pelican has a store, a few cafes, steam bath, small library and Rosie's Bar and Grill. A cold storage processes products from the sea.

The town started in the early 1940s as the dream of Kalle Raatikainen. For years in the 1930s Raatikainen had been anchoring his fish-buying scows in many of the coves still used by buyers today. He felt it would be easier to have a processing plant closer to the fishing grounds. After a thorough search, Raatikainen chose the site of present-day Pelican — a name he took from his diesel-powered boat.

The other year-round community within the service area of Sitka is another fishing village, Elfin Cove (population 28). This protected anchorage has a narrow opening into Cross Sound and is near the largest offshore salmon fishing banks in Southeast Alaska, the Fairweather Grounds. A fish-buying barge ices salmon for shipment to processing plants elsewhere in Southeast Alaska. This process is a continuation of the activity which led to the founding of Elfin Cove. Fish buyers mild-cured salmon here starting around 1927. A modest store operates in Elfin Cove during fishing season, and when the season ends the 28 permanent residents find the cove a quiet spot during the long winter.

Left — A narrow boardwalk runs along the waterfront at Elfin Cove, providing a place for quiet and picturesque strolls through town.
(Chip Porter)

Elfin Cove was founded on the fishing industry, which through the years has remained the mainstay of the economy. Here, many of the community's fishing boats find the Inner Harbor a snug place to keep out of the wind.
(Chip Porter)

ALASKA GEOGRAPHIC® back issues

The North Slope, Vol. 1, No. 1. Charter issue. Out of print.

One Man's Wilderness, Vol. 1, No. 2. Out of print.

Admiralty . . . Island in Contention, Vol. 1, No. 3. $7.50.

Fisheries of the North Pacific: History, Species, Gear & Processes, Vol. 1, No. 4. Out of print.

The Alaska-Yukon Wild Flowers Guide, Vol. 2, No. 1. Out of print.

Richard Harrington's Yukon, Vol. 2, No. 2. Out of print.

Prince William Sound, Vol. 2, No. 3. Out of print.

Yakutat: The Turbulent Crescent, Vol. 2, No. 4. Out of print.

Glacier Bay: Old Ice, New Land, Vol. 3, No. 1. Out of print.

The Land: Eye of the Storm, Vol. 3, No. 2. Out of print.

Richard Harrington's Antarctic, Vol. 3, No. 3. $12.95.

The Silver Years of the Alaska Canned Salmon Industry: An Album of Historical Photos, Vol. 3, No. 4. $17.95.

Alaska's Volcanoes: Northern Link In the Ring of Fire, Vol. 4, No. 1. Out of print.

The Brooks Range: Environmental Watershed, Vol. 4, No. 2. Out of print.

Kodiak: Island of Change, Vol. 4, No. 3. Out of print.

Wilderness Proposals: Which Way for Alaska's Lands?, Vol. 4, No. 4. Out of print.

Cook Inlet Country, Vol. 5, No. 1. Out of print.

Southeast: Alaska's Panhandle, Vol. 5, No. 2. $19.95.

Bristol Bay Basin, Vol. 5, No. 3. Out of print.

Alaska Whales and Whaling, Vol. 5, No. 4. $19.95.

Yukon-Kuskokwim Delta, Vol. 6, No. 1. Out of print.

Aurora Borealis, Vol. 6, No. 2. $14.95.

Alaska's Native People, Vol. 6, No. 3. $24.95.

The Stikine River, Vol. 6, No. 4. $12.95.

Alaska's Great Interior, Vol. 7, No. 1. $17.95.

A Photographic Geography of Alaska, Vol. 7, No. 2. $17.95.

The Aleutians, Vol. 7, No. 3. $19.95.

Klondike Lost: A Decade of Photographs by Kinsey & Kinsey, Vol. 7, No. 4. Out of print.

Wrangell-Saint Elias, Vol. 8, No. 1. $19.95.

Alaska Mammals, Vol. 8, No. 2. $15.95.

The Kotzebue Basin, Vol. 8, No. 3. $15.95.

Alaska National Interest Lands, Vol. 8, No. 4. $17.95.

Alaska's Glaciers, Vol. 9, No. 1. $19.95

Sitka and Its Ocean/Island World, Vol. 9, No. 2. $19.95.

Islands of the Seals: The Pribilofs, Vol. 9, No. 3. $12.95.

Alaska's Oil/Gas & Minerals Industry, Vol. 9, No. 4. $15.95.

Adventure Roads North: The Story of the Alaska Highway and Other Roads in *The MILEPOST*, Vol. 10, No. 1. $17.95.

Anchorage and the Cook Inlet Basin, Vol. 10, No. 2. $17.95.

Alaska's Salmon Fisheries, Vol. 10, No. 3. $15.95.

Up the Koyukuk, Vol. 10, No. 4. $17.95.

Nome: City of the Golden Beaches, Vol. 11, No. 1. $14.95.

Alaska's Farms and Gardens, Vol. 11, No. 2. $15.95.

Chilkat River Valley, Vol. 11, No. 3. $15.95.

Alaska Steam, Vol. 11, No. 4. $14.95.

Northwest Territories, Vol. 12, No. 1. $17.95.

Alaska's Forest Resources, Vol. 12, No. 2. $16.95.

Alaska Native Arts and Crafts, Vol. 12, No. 3. $17.95.

Our Arctic Year, Vol. 12, No. 4. $15.95.

Where Mountains Meet the Sea: Alaska's Gulf Coast, Vol. 13, No. 1. $17.95.

Backcountry Alaska, Vol. 13, No. 2. $17.95.

British Columbia's Coast: The Canadian Inside Passage, Vol. 13, No. 3. $17.95.

Lake Clark/Lake Iliamna Country, Vol. 13, No. 4. Out of print.

Dogs of the North, Vol. 14, No. 1. $17.95.

South/Southeast Alaska, Vol. 14, No. 2. Out of print.

Alaska's Seward Peninsula, Vol. 14, No. 3. $15.95.

The Upper Yukon Basin, Vol. 14, No. 4. $17.95.

Glacier Bay: Icy Wilderness, Vol. 15, No. 1. $16.95.

Dawson City, Vol. 15, No. 2. $15.95.

Denali, Vol. 15, No. 3. $16.95.

The Kuskokwim River, Vol. 15, No. 4. $17.95.

Katmai Country, Vol. 16, No. 1. $17.95

North Slope Now, Vol. 16, No. 2. $14.95.

The Tanana Basin, Vol. 16, No. 3. $17.95.

The Copper Trail, Vol. 16, No. 4. $17.95.

The Nushagak Basin, Vol. 17, No. 1. $17.95.

Juneau, Vol. 17, No. 2. $17.95.

The Middle Yukon River, Vol. 17, No. 3. $17.95.

The Lower Yukon River, Vol. 17, No. 4. $17.95.

ALL PRICES SUBJECT TO CHANGE.

Your $39 membership in The Alaska Geographic Society includes four subsequent issues of *ALASKA GEOGRAPHIC*®, the Society's official quarterly. Please add $4 for non-U.S. memberships.

Additional membership information is available upon request. Single copies of the *ALASKA GEOGRAPHIC*® back issues are also available. When ordering, please make payments in U.S. funds and add $1.50 postage/handling per copy. Non-U.S. postage extra. To order back issues send your check or money order and volumes desired to:

The Alaska Geographic Society

P.O. Box 93370, Anchorage, AK 99509